Population

Opposing Viewpoints®

Population

Opposing Viewpoints®

Other Books of Related Interest

Population

Opposing Viewpoints®

Karen F. Balkin, *Book Editor*

Bruce Glassman, *Vice President*
Bonnie Szumski, *Publisher*
Helen Cothran, *Managing Editor*

OPPOSING
VIEWPOINTS®
SERIES

GREENHAVEN PRESS

An imprint of Thomson Gale, a part of The Thomson Corporation

THOMSON
━━━━━✳━━━━━ ™
GALE

Detroit • New York • San Francisco • San Diego • New Haven, Conn.
Waterville, Maine • London • Munich

LIBRARY OF CONGRESS CATALOGING-IN-PUBLICATION DATA

Population / Karen F. Balkin, book editor.
   p. cm. — (Opposing viewpoints series)
Includes bibliographical references and index.
ISBN 0-7377-2951-1 (lib. : alk. paper) — ISBN 0-7377-2952-X (pbk. : alk. paper)
   1. Population. 2. Population policy. 3. Demographic transition—Economic aspects. 4. Age distribution (Demography)—Economic aspects. 5. Emigration and immigration—Economic aspects—United States. I. Balkin, Karen F., 1949– . II. Opposing viewpoints series (Unnumbered)
HB871.P6296 2005
363.9—dc22
                                 2004060862

Printed in the United States of America

JUN – – 2006

"Congress shall make
no law. . . abridging the
freedom of speech, or of
the press."

First Amendment to the U.S. Constitution

The basic foundation of our democracy is the First
Amendment guarantee of freedom of expression.
The Opposing Viewpoints Series is dedicated to the
concept of this basic freedom and the idea that it is
more important to practice it than to enshrine it.

Contents

Why Consider Opposing Viewpoints?

"The only way in which a human being can make some approach to knowing the whole of a subject is by hearing what can be said about it by persons of every variety of opinion and studying all modes in which it can be looked at by every character of mind. No wise man ever acquired his wisdom in any mode but this."

John Stuart Mill

In our media-intensive culture it is not difficult to find differing opinions. Thousands of newspapers and magazines and dozens of radio and television talk shows resound with differing points of view. The difficulty lies in deciding which opinion to agree with and which "experts" seem the most credible. The more inundated we become with differing opinions and claims, the more essential it is to hone critical reading and thinking skills to evaluate these ideas. Opposing Viewpoints books address this problem directly by presenting stimulating debates that can be used to enhance and teach these skills. The varied opinions contained in each book examine many different aspects of a single issue. While examining these conveniently edited opposing views, readers can develop critical thinking skills such as the ability to compare and contrast authors' credibility, facts, argumentation styles, use of persuasive techniques, and other stylistic tools. In short, the Opposing Viewpoints Series is an ideal way to attain the higher-level thinking and reading skills so essential in a culture of diverse and contradictory opinions.

In addition to providing a tool for critical thinking, Opposing Viewpoints books challenge readers to question their own strongly held opinions and assumptions. Most people form their opinions on the basis of upbringing, peer pressure, and personal, cultural, or professional bias. By reading carefully balanced opposing views, readers must directly confront new ideas as well as the opinions of those with whom they disagree. This is not to simplistically argue that everyone who reads opposing views will—or should—change his or her opinion. Instead, the series enhances readers' understanding of their own views by encouraging confrontation with opposing ideas. Careful examination of others' views can lead to the readers' understanding of the logical inconsistencies in their own opinions, perspective on why they hold an opinion, and the consideration of the possibility that their opinion requires further evaluation.

Evaluating Other Opinions

To ensure that this type of examination occurs, Opposing Viewpoints books present all types of opinions. Prominent spokespeople on different sides of each issue as well as well-known professionals from many disciplines challenge the reader. An additional goal of the series is to provide a forum for other, less known, or even unpopular viewpoints. The opinion of an ordinary person who has had to make the decision to cut off life support from a terminally ill relative, for example, may be just as valuable and provide just as much insight as a medical ethicist's professional opinion. The editors have two additional purposes in including these less known views. One, the editors encourage readers to respect others' opinions—even when not enhanced by professional credibility. It is only by reading or listening to and objectively evaluating others' ideas that one can determine whether they are worthy of consideration. Two, the inclusion of such viewpoints encourages the important critical thinking skill of objectively evaluating an author's credentials and bias. This evaluation will illuminate an author's reasons for taking a particular stance on an issue and will aid in readers' evaluation of the author's ideas.

It is our hope that these books will give readers a deeper understanding of the issues debated and an appreciation of the complexity of even seemingly simple issues when good and honest people disagree. This awareness is particularly important in a democratic society such as ours in which people enter into public debate to determine the common good. Those with whom one disagrees should not be regarded as enemies but rather as people whose views deserve careful examination and may shed light on one's own.

Thomas Jefferson once said that "difference of opinion leads to inquiry, and inquiry to truth." Jefferson, a broadly educated man, argued that "if a nation expects to be ignorant and free . . . it expects what never was and never will be." As individuals and as a nation, it is imperative that we consider the opinions of others and examine them with skill and discernment. The Opposing Viewpoints Series is intended to help readers achieve this goal.

David L. Bender and Bruno Leone,
Founders

Greenhaven Press anthologies primarily consist of previously published material taken from a variety of sources, including periodicals, books, scholarly journals, newspapers, government documents, and position papers from private and public organizations. These original sources are often edited for length and to ensure their accessibility for a young adult audience. The anthology editors also change the original titles of these works in order to clearly present the main thesis of each viewpoint and to explicitly indicate the opinion presented in the viewpoint. These alterations are made in consideration of both the reading and comprehension levels of a young adult audience. Every effort is made to ensure that Greenhaven Press accurately reflects the original intent of the authors included in this anthology.

Introduction

"The most important changes in world population over the next fifty years are less likely to be in the total number of people than in their age and geographic location."

—*Don Peck*, Atlantic Monthly, *October 2002*

Many demographers today argue that the aging of developed nations' populations will, more than absolute population size, determine the world's future. Peter G. Peterson, author of *Gray Dawn: How the Coming Age Wave Will Transform America—and the World* says, "Global aging will become not just the transcendent economic issue of the twenty-first century, but the transcendent political issue as well." At stake is the world's distribution of wealth and power. As the populations of developed nations—which have traditionally been the most affluent and powerful—age and contract, the populations of developing nations—which have been the poorest and least powerful—continue to grow. The fastest growing countries are the least developed: India, China, Pakistan, Nigeria, Bangladesh, and Indonesia. Developed nations, such as the United States and most European countries, have populations that are rapidly aging. Over 19 percent of the people in developed nations are over sixty years of age. As more of the world's human capital continues to build in developing nations, many experts predict that power and money will flow to these countries as well, upsetting a decades-old balance of power.

Low fertility rates and longer life spans—mostly due to advances in public health and medical technology—are responsible for the aging populations of the United States and most European nations. In developed countries, the growing elderly population will create a precipitous drop in the ratio of working-age people to nonworking, dependent individuals. For example, by 2050, there will be just three Italians of working age for every two over sixty-five. Throughout Europe, only 57 percent of the population will be of working age, compared to about 63 percent worldwide.

Reductions in both the relative size of the working population and the overall population size in developed countries could result in major political and economic changes. For example, demographers and political scientists predict that the United States and Europe will have to devote increasingly larger portions of their gross domestic product to the care of the elderly while the least developed countries will be able to use proportionally more of their resources for economic investment and capital growth. With more of their resources going toward elder care, the developed countries will have less to spend on defense and domestic and global security programs. Peterson argues, "Falling birthrates, together with a rising demand for young workers, will also inevitably mean smaller armies. And how many parents will allow their only child to go off to war?" With less money to spend on defense and security, developed nations will be newly vulnerable. Conversely, poor nations will likely get richer, and in turn more powerful. Peterson says. "A quarter century from now, will the divide between today's 'rich' and 'poor' nations be better described as a divide between growth and decline, surplus and deficit, expansion and retreat, future and past?"

One factor that may affect this development is immigration. Many pro-immigration advocates see immigrants as the demographic saviors of developed countries. These analysts maintain that immigrants, typically among the youngest and poorest of the world's people, can provide the youthful workers that aging nations need to maintain their productivity. According to Daniel T. Griswold, director of the Cato Institute's Center for Trade Policy Studies, "Without immigration [America's] labor force would begin to shrink within two decades. . . . Immigrants could help revitalize demographically declining areas of the country, just as they helped revitalize New York City and other previously declining urban centers."

Anti-immigration and population control advocates, however, maintain that the United States will be better off economically and ecologically if immigration is curtailed. They argue that a smaller, albeit older, U.S. population will ensure a more prosperous and secure future for everyone. David Simcox, chairman of the board of the Center for Immigration Studies, a Washington, D.C., think tank, argues, "Immigrants and their U.S.-born children now account for 60 percent of U.S. population growth. . . . Each expansion of already high immigration adds to the momentum that is leaving behind the limits that an environmentally safe and sustainable U.S. population demands."

Authors in *Opposing Viewpoints: Population* debate the importance of population and demographics in the following chapters: Is There a Population Problem? What Problems Are Associated with Population Growth? What Are the Effects of Immigration on America's Population? What Population Policies Should Be Pursued? The continued growth of developing countries' populations and the aging of shrinking populations in America and Europe present demographic, social, and political problems the world has never known before. Power shifts and policy changes are inevitable as the world adjusts to these new demographics.

CHAPTER 1

Is There a Population Problem?

Chapter Preface

In 1980 economist Julian Simon and biologist Paul Ehrlich bet on the likelihood of population growth negatively affecting the availability of nonrenewable resources such as metals. They wagered whether the market price, adjusted for inflation, of five industrial metals would increase or decrease by 1990. Simon argued that the price of the metals would decrease—they would become less scarce—because their importance to industry would inspire entrepreneurs to either find new natural sources or develop replacements. Ehrlich insisted that, like all nonrenewable resources being rapidly depleted by the increasing needs of a growing population, the metals would become scarcer and thus more expensive. Simon won the bet—the metals decreased in price by an average of 40 percent during the ten-year term of the wager, thus proving that they did not become scarcer. The importance of the wager, however, is not the absolute price of industrial metals. The bet's significance lies in what it says about the consequences of population growth.

Simon's argument that even a rapidly growing population does not create any problems it cannot solve is optimistic and compelling. His thesis is that humans are the ultimate resource. "Human beings," he writes, "are not just more mouths to feed, but are productive and inventive minds that help find creative solutions to man's problems, thus leaving us better off over the long run." He maintains that life on Earth has steadily improved and will continue to get better no matter how large the population.

In contrast, Ehrlich, author of the controversial book *The Population Bomb*, argues that a rapidly growing population creates unsolvable ecological problems. He maintains that developed countries such as the United States have been particularly destructive to the environment. Ehrlich argues, "We've already had too much economic growth in the United States. Economic growth in countries like ours is the disease, not the cure." While his prediction in the 1960s that worldwide starvation due to ecological disasters would occur in the 1970s and 1980s never came to pass, his theory that overpopulation is causing natural resources to become scarcer is widely accepted.

Simon and Ehrlich offer opposite arguments on the effect of population on nonrenewable resources. This is just one of the issues that the authors in the following chapter explore as they debate whether population is a problem in the twenty-first century.

"Overpopulation will become the 'plague of the 21st century.'"

Overpopulation Is a Serious Problem

Frosty Wooldridge

Overpopulation is rapidly depleting the earth's resources, Frosty Wooldridge contends in the following viewpoint. In the United States overpopulation has resulted in traffic congestion, poverty, and environmental devastation, he claims. Wooldridge warns that failure to control population now will result in horrific population problems for future generations. Frosty Wooldridge is a teacher and population activist. He is also the author of *Incursion into America: Immigration's Unarmed Invasion—Deadly Consequences*.

As you read, consider the following questions:

1. According to Wooldridge, how many people are added to the U.S. population every year?
2. Name two of the consequences the author argues are the result of overpopulation.
3. Which three countries does Wooldridge argue ignored their population problem until they were unsolvable?

Albert Einstein wrote, "The problems that exist in the world today cannot be solved by the level of thinking that created them." Nonetheless, governors, our president, Congress and other leaders stagger forward with 'solutions' that accelerate America's population problems.

In the past 10 years, the world added 880 million people. America added 33 million and California added six million—on its way from 35 million to 55 million in the next 30 years. Like California, many states found themselves inundated with sprawl, gridlock, rising home prices, new forms of crime and diseases. Today, America stands at 292 million and grows by 3.3 million per year. Just past the mid-century, America will add 200 million people.

Dwindling Resources

Soon past the mid-century, those added millions will be struggling for dwindling resources, water, food and a diminishing quality of life. In western states like California and Arizona, a drought in 2050 will become a *disaster* along with many other consequences.

For graphic examples, one need only look at India and China. In a recent speech, Arun Gandhi, grandson of Mahatma Gandhi, said, "In my country, 4 million people are born in the streets, live in the streets and die in the streets—never having used a toilet or shower." If massive population is so good, why is India so poor?

Overpopulation will become the 'plague of the 21st century.'

Where is America headed? Do we want such a legacy for our own children? According to *60 Minutes*, we have one million homeless children struggling in our inner cities today. What will be the fate of another 200 million people who create homeless children? How many are too many and when will Americans address that fact? Which leader?

At this time—no one. Politicians scurry like cockroaches at the mention of population stabilization. Corporations demand larger markets as if nonrenewable resources will appear out of a magician's black hat. We're like a runaway freight train with no brakes headed toward the edge of the Grand Canyon.

Americans face consequences in every corner of our nation. Our East and West coasts, teeming with too many people, strive to deal with escalating water, air and land dilemmas. Acid rains pound our lakes with chemicals. Our cities create thick clouds where millions of children breathe carcinogens with every breath. Farmers kill microbes in the soil with fertilizers and pesticides—leaving us with contaminated foods for eating. Each year, 1.3 million new cancers are detected in our US citizens—an epidemic of our own making.

Locher. © 1994 by the *Chicago Tribune*. Reproduced by permission.

Eleanor Roosevelt said it 50 years ago; "We must prevent human tragedy rather than run around trying to save ourselves after an event has already occurred. Unfortunately, history clearly shows that we arrive at catastrophe by failing to meet the situation, by failing to act when we should have acted. The opportunity passes us by and the next disaster is always more difficult and compounded than the last one."

Immediate Action Is Necessary

By failing to act now, what kinds of consequences will we as a nation face when we hit ½ billion people? In the US with 200 million more people, that's 77% more traffic, 77% added planes in the air, 77% increased pollution, 77% faster uses of already limited resources like water and gasoline. With each new added American, 1 to 12.6 acres of wilderness is plowed up to support that person. In the next 10 years, according to the National Academy of Sciences, 2,500 plants and animals will become extinct in the USA because of habitat destruction via population growth. Why aren't we addressing the moral and biological consequences of such horrific extinction rates?

When you add global warming, ocean fisheries collapsing, acid rain, ozone destruction, drought, contaminated water supplies, poisoning and sterilization of the soils by insecticides and fertilizers—we're building unimaginable consequences.

How serious is our problem? Upon receiving the Sanger Award for Human Rights in 1966, Dr. Martin Luther King said, ". . . the plague of overpopulation is soluble by means we have discovered and with resources we possess. What is lacking is not sufficient knowledge of the solution, but universal consciousness of the gravity of the problems and the education of billions of people who are its victims."

Immigration Must Be Controlled

Fifty years ago, Bangladesh, India and China ignored their accelerating populations. Today, their problems are so gargantuan, they can't solve them. As if like lemmings, America's leaders follow the same steps. According to the Center for Immigration Studies, we're allowing the immigration of more than 2.3 million people annually from countries that refuse family planning. Since the American female has a fertility rate of 2.03 children, it's not Americans causing the rising population tide. We need immigration reform and reduction to less than 175,000 people annually before population momentum forces us into an unsustainable society. If we don't tame this 'immigration monster,' it will grow past our ability to manage it.

If we do nothing, we commit our children and all living things to a difficult future by not addressing overpopulation in 2003. It's a disservice to ourselves, our nation and future generations.

"We will not run out of food, natural resources, or room. The theory is completely and dangerously false."

Overpopulation Is a Myth

Austin Ruse

Austin Ruse argues in the following viewpoint that the theory that the earth is overpopulated is completely false. He maintains that there is plenty of food and resources for the world's population. Ruse insists that the real problem is declining birthrates, which are creating societies in which the elderly outnumber the young, seriously straining social services. Austin Ruse is president of the Catholic Family and Human Rights Institute, a nongovernmental organization that monitors UN activity.

As you read, consider the following questions:
1. What is eugenics, according to the author?
2. What does Ruse argue is the chief feature of the population bomb theory?
3. In the author's opinion, why did UNFPA decide to limit its activities in China?

The claim that the world will become dangerously over-populated has never been true. It was false when first postulated in the 19th century. It was false when *The Population Bomb* was first published in the 1960s. It is false now. That this theory is still taught in grade schools all over the world even today does not make it any truer. It remains a false theory.

In this essay I will briefly trace the development through time of the oddly utopian idea that human misery can end with the end of humanity, or at least the end of a good portion of it. I will address the work of one of the theory's most important proponents, the United Nations Population Fund. I will discuss the differences between the feminist wing and the pure population control wing of the movement. And finally I will explain more fully how and why the theory of overpopulation is not true.

Malthusianism Beginnings

This war on the concept of people is now more than a century old. It has moved through four distinct but closely related stages: Malthusianism, eugenics, the population bomb, and is now in the stage known as "reproductive rights."

Malthusianism, named for the early 19th century scientist Thomas Malthus, posited that having too many people in the world is the inevitable cause of many maladies, among them, hunger, starvation, disease, and war. The theory suggests that the population of the world grows exponentially while food production doesn't, with the inevitable result of massive starvation. Not thoroughly discredited until the advent of modern farming techniques in the 20th century, Malthusianism has provided the intellectual underpinnings of all the other iterations of population theory.

The next step in the movement came with the advent of eugenics, the theory that not all races are the same and that the "bad" races must die out to make room for the "good" ones. The "bad" races generally corresponded with those who were poorer and darker than the proponents of eugenics. Early proponents of this theory included Margaret Sanger, the founder of Planned Parenthood who openly expressed racist beliefs and who was admired by the Nazi regime (these facts are ignored by Sanger's ideological and biological heirs).

The Population Bomb Theory

Of course, the Nazi regime gave eugenics its properly bad name so population theory went underground, gussied itself up and reemerged in the 1950s with the imprimatur of the American political and academic establishment. It came with a new name—the population explosion—which harkened back to the work of Malthus, but still targeted darker skinned populations in the developing world. Instead of simply saying the world would run out of food, it now posited that the world would run out of nearly everything including food, natural resources and eventually room to walk around in. This "population bomb" theory drove the movement through the 1960s until the early '90s and even beyond.

The chief feature of the population bomb scare has been coercion. If, as proponents suggested, overpopulation was a dire threat to the entire planet, then policy makers believed that some populations must be forced to reduce their number.

Almost always, coercion comes from the hands of governments directed at their own people. The most famous examples of coercion occur in developing world countries like China and Peru. The cases of coercion there are well documented and very obvious. Women in these countries were given abortions against their will. Others were sterilized without their knowledge. Still others were bribed with food and medicine in exchange for abortion and sterilization. These instances occur mostly in the developing world, but even in the United States there are well publicized cases in which poor, drug addicted women are paid cash by private groups for getting sterilized.

While coercion occurs mostly at the hands of poor governments on their own poor people, the impetus for it comes from rich western countries, chiefly the United States and those in the European Union, but also from various international institutions, most notably the United Nations.

The United States government helped to found the UN Fund for Population Activities (UNFPA) in 1969 to be a nonpartisan clearinghouse for population and demographic information. UNFPA, however, quickly evolved into an advocacy group that has had a hand in more than one coercive population control program. Within ten years of its founding, for instance, UNFPA assisted in the establishment of the most brutal population control program the world has ever seen.

With the direct help of UNFPA the Chinese government instituted a policy that forbade women from having more than one child in their lifetime. Some women who tried to have more than one child were forced into having abortions. Others were fined to such a high degree for a second pregnancy they had no choice but to have an abortion. Indeed, according to *The Washington Post*, in just the first six years of the program, 50 million forced abortions occurred in China.

UNFPA Limited Its Activities

Under threat of losing U.S. financial assistance, UNFPA eventually promised to limit its activities to only 32 Chinese counties and promised that all forms of coercion in those counties would end (this even though UNFPA denied that any coercion existed at all). UNFPA further promised that if coercion still existed in any of those 32 counties they would leave China altogether. In 2002 the U.S. government determined that coercion still existed in those 32 counties, that UNFPA was complicit in providing technical assistance, and promptly withdrew financial support. UNFPA still denies coercion exists in the 32 counties and UNFPA continues to publicly praise the Chinese one-child policy.

China is not the only place where UNFPA has been proven to assist in coercion. Not long ago the Peruvian government led by former President Fujimori pursued a very aggressive population control program against native peasant women. U.S. government investigators found that these women were tricked into sterilizations under the guise of other procedures. Other women were withheld food until they agreed to sterilizations. UNFPA was a financier of the Peruvian program, and the forced and coerced sterilizations occurred in UNFPA facilities. Though UNFPA denied coercion existed in the Peruvian program, they commissioned a study that confirmed for them that coercion did exist in the program. UNFPA's response to its own negative report was to bury it and lie about it. As recently as the summer of 2002 UNFPA denied the existence of the report, which had been unearthed by a Peruvian journalist.

Fertility Rates Are Falling

The world is over-populated and heading towards demographic catastrophe, right?

Wrong. According to Max Singer, writing in *The Atlantic Monthly* of August 1999, "Unless people's values change greatly, several centuries from now there could be fewer people living in the entire world than live in the United States today." How does he come to this startling and unorthodox view? Simply because no demographer predicted that when fertility dropped to replacement level—which is 2.1 child per woman per lifetime—it would keep falling. But it has. . . .

In the 1960s, population grew at 2 per cent. It's now growing at 1 per cent and if it continues to drop as the pattern suggests it will, it will head into negative numbers. Many demographers now think the world's population will peak at 8 billion within fifty years or so, and then go into a rapid decline. So far from facing a population explosion, we're more likely looking at a population implosion.

Antonia Feitz, *Enter Stage Right—A Journal of Modern Conservatism*, May 8, 2000.

At the time that these debates raged during the 1990s the population controllers once more began to change their terms. They determined, quite correctly, that population control was getting bad press. It was viewed as too "top down," in the words of population control advocates. In addition to the bad press, population control advocates also began receiving reports from their own demographers, which presented startling information: the drive to slow population growth by discouraging fertility was becoming more successful than anyone could imagine.

Though not revealed to the general public until the late 1990s, it was becoming obvious to demographic experts by the time of the Cairo Conference on Population and Development in 1994, that fertility rates were plummeting rapidly all over the world. I will address the facts in a minute but first will point out the switch in terminology, which exists to the present day.

Reproductive Rights

First, they determined that the top down approach and the phrase "population control" were no longer tenable. Second, they already knew or suspected that fertility rates were plummeting and they feared that policy makers would conclude that population control was no longer necessary. Third, they wanted fertility rates and, therefore, population control to continue to decline. Their solution to these sticky problems was to cloak the old theory of overpopulation in the language of human rights, the political argument *par excellence* of the late 20th century. Enter the phrase "reproductive rights." The thinking went that if everyone demanded and received their "reproductive rights," as defined by the UN, then fertility rates would continue to decline. So, under the guidance and support of UNFPA, the United Nations began the international call for reproductive rights at the Cairo Conference on Population and Development in 1994.

Here we have entered the latest but certainly not the last phase of the war against the concept of people. It started in Malthusianism, continued in eugenics, switched to the population explosion and has ended up, at least for now, in the fight for reproductive rights. And here we enter briefly the dichotomy in their movement, that between the feminists and the population controllers.

Actually the split is not all that great. Some feminists, though not many, have considered population control as an assault against women. Some of them, though very few, spoke out against the Chinese one-child policy. And none of them spoke out against coercion in Peru. But at least theoretically there is a dichotomy between those who believe that women's rights lie in the advancement of abortion yet who still criticize coercion in family planning and those who believe so strongly in the necessity of population control that women's rights may be trampled as a consequence. This final phase of the anti-people movement uses the language of women's rights in the service of population control.

Let me finish with how I began. The theory that the world

is so awash in people that it will eventually die is false and it always has been. We will not run out of food, natural resources, or room. The theory is completely and dangerously false. The world now produces more food on less land than ever before. The world is awash in food. The problem is getting it to the hungry. Starvation occurs in the world today not from lack of food but generally as a result of bad policies or the use of starvation as a tool of war. Also, the cost of natural resources is now lower than forty years ago. Price is always a marker for availability: lower prices mean greater availability. Why are natural resources more plentiful? Simply because of our ingenuity. Mankind is better at getting natural resources out of the ground, whatever they are, and we are more efficient in their use.

Better Health and Longer Life

Still, the population continues to grow. How can that be? For a very good reason. According to Harvard's Nicholas Eberstadt, it is not that people "reproduce like bunnies" rather that they "no longer die like flies." The most startling revolution in the most revolutionary 20th century was one of health. Where a century ago, almost any disease could kill someone in a matter of days, these diseases are now routinely cured. Where once someone could hope to live into the 60s, they now routinely live well into the 70s, 80s, and even 90s.

The fact is that the much feared fertility rate began declining in the West more than 150 years ago, long before the advent of UN-style family planning and population control. In fact, France reached what is called the demographic transition in the 19th century. The fact of nature is that fertility rates decline naturally when populations move from the farm to the city and from agricultural subsistence to the industrial age. They decline also as women move toward education and postpone marriage, also aspects of modernization.

It turns out the war on fertility was not necessary and what we have achieved in artificially lowering it is a problem the world has never seen. At this point more than 80 countries have achieved what is known as below replacement fertility, the point at which women are having so few children, generally thought to be below 2.1 children per woman, that countries are no longer replacing themselves. The UN predicts that every nation on earth, with the exception of a few African nations, will reach below replacement fertility within the next twenty years. And this is a very serious problem. What this means is a rapidly aging population that turns the demographic pyramid on its head. Societies are meant to have lots of young people supporting an ever-shrinking number of old people. Below replacement fertility has meant in many countries there are more old people than young people. Fifteen years ago Japan reached a global first; it reached the point where it had more people over 65 than under 15. This is a recipe for economic disaster and inter-generational warfare over levels of government taxation and spending for social services for the elderly. The UN now acknowledges this.

The Beginning of Population Decline

In recent years, the UN Population Division (official UN statistical analysts) has sounded the alarm about below replacement fertility. [In 2002] it hosted an expert meeting at which demographers from all over the world concluded they did not know how low fertility can go. The UN now believes the world population will top out at roughly 8 billion people in 2050 and then begin to decline.

The population controllers continue to make their case, however. They still say the world will soon starve, and that we will soon run out of natural resources, and that the planet is running out of room. Anyone can test the theory, however. Next time you are in an airplane flying virtually anywhere in the world, even in the very populous United States, look down from on high and what you will see is a remarkably empty planet straining to be made a garden by more of us.

VIEWPOINT

"Our species, unlike all others, can use problem-solving techniques to expand resources."

Science Will Solve the Population Problem

Nicholas Eberstadt

Nicholas Eberstadt argues in the following viewpoint that scientific discoveries and technological developments will allow human beings to save themselves from the consequences of overpopulation. Along with careful conservation, continued breakthroughs in health, agriculture, and contraception will make it possible for people to increase the carrying capacity of the earth, he contends. Nicholas Eberstadt holds the Henry Wendt Chair in Political Economy at the American Enterprise Institute, a conservative public policy research organization.

As you read, consider the following questions:
1. What biological law, described by T.R. Malthus, governs every form of life on Earth except human beings, in the author's opinion?
2. What does Eberstadt argue is responsible for the unprecedented population explosion of the twentieth century?
3. What does the author maintain has happened to patterns of economic activity around the globe in the past century?

Nicholas Eberstadt, "We've Got Lots of Room for People," *The American Enterprise*, vol. 11, December 2000. Copyright © 2000 by the American Enterprise Institute for Public Policy Research. Reprinted with permission of *The American Enterprise*, a magazine of Politics, Business, and Culture. On the Web at www.TAEmag.com.

The notion that human beings, through their growing numbers and their escalating levels of consumption, are outstripping the globe's capacity to sustain them is one of the most powerful economic claims of the modern era. Ever since T.R. Malthus first made these arguments in a famous 1798 treatise, many people have been persuaded that a serious "population problem" is imminent and requires immediate action.

The durability of this notion is understandable, because it sounds so plausible. The planet, after all, is of a fixed size, and at some point a finite sphere will necessarily be unable to meet a geometrically rising demand upon its resources. Moreover, every other form of life on earth is governed by the immutable and unforgiving biological laws Malthus described: the regular tendency for a species to procreate beyond its environment's capacity to feed it, only to have its numbers brought back to "equilibrium" through brutal spikes in the death rate.

Life Expectancy Has Increased

Yet human beings are not like other animals. Our species, unlike all others, can use problem-solving techniques to expand resources. Beasts cannot purposely transform their survival prospects. Human beings can—and they have done so dramatically, across the entire planet.

In 1900, the expected lifespan for men and women around the world probably averaged about 30 years. Today, according to projections by the U.N., it is probably over 65 years, and in the places conventionally deemed most prone to Malthusian calamity, improvements in longevity have been especially striking. During the past half-century, according to the U.N.'s figures, life expectancy for the low-income countries known as the "less developed regions" has jumped by well over 23 years, or more than half. During that same period, the overall infant mortality rate for the poorer countries is believed to have fallen by almost two-thirds. Humanity, in short, is in the midst of a "health explosion," which entirely accounts for the unprecedented "population explosion" of the twentieth century.

These tremendous and sustained worldwide improvements in human health speak to another crucial distinction between our species and all other animals. For the same factors that have made our health revolution possible—advances in scientific knowledge, the spread of education, improvements in organizational technique, and the like—have also supported a spectacular, and continuing, increase in human productivity.

Consider the race between population and food over the course of the twentieth century. Traditional Malthusian doctrine maintains that food production cannot keep pace with mankind's ability to multiply. The twentieth century should have provided a test case for that proposition, since between 1900 and 2000 the world's population nearly quadrupled, surging from perhaps 1.6 billion to over 6 billion.

More and Better Food

Yet this extraordinary population explosion did not consign humanity to mounting hunger. Just the opposite: Mankind enjoys a far better diet today than it did when the earth's population was only one-fourth as large.

To be sure, millions upon millions of people still live under the threat of deadly hunger. Yet such tragic circumstances are now, finally, the distinct exception rather than the rule of the human condition. The inescapable fact is that humanity has never before been as well fed as today—and our improvements in nutritional well-being coincided with the most massive and rapid increase in population in human experience. In fact, despite our species' exponentially increasing demand for food, there is compelling evidence that foodstuffs are actually growing ever less scarce. . . .

Real prices for [corn, wheat, and rice] have plummeted by over 70 percent since 1900. These declines in prices were not smooth, but the temporary upswings in food costs were mainly the result of political disruptions—World War I, World War II, the Korean War, and the government-exacerbated "world food crisis" of the early 1970s—rather than environmental or demographic events.

The long-term fall in cereal prices is an important way to gauge the availability of food in the modern world. Since prices measure scarcity, falling prices mean foodstuffs are significantly less scarce at the end of the twentieth century than they were at its beginning—even though mankind is now consuming far more of them today.

The facts are undeniable: Global population has been rising at an average pace of about 1.3 percent a year for a century, and global cereal prices have simultaneously been falling nearly 1.3 percent per year. Never have more people inhabited the world than today—and never before has food been so abundantly available.

Human Intelligence and Technology Will Triumph

A reading of economic and social history quickly makes one thing plain: Throughout history people have thought they saw overpopulation. Even the great nineteenth century social scientist W. Stanley Jevons in 1865 claimed that England's industrial expansion would soon cease due to the exhaustion of the country's coal supply. However, as shortages developed, prices rose. The profit motive stimulated entrepreneurs to find new sources, to develop better technology for finding and extracting coal, and to transport it to where it was needed. The crisis never happened. Today, the USA has proven reserves sufficient to last hundreds or thousands of years. If one resource does begin to run low, rising prices will encourage a switch to alternatives. Certainly, even a vastly bloated population cannot hope to exhaust energy supplies. (Solar energy and power from nuclear fission and soon fusion are practically endless.) So long as we have plentiful energy we can produce substitute resources and even generate more of existing resources, including food. Even if population continues to grow well beyond 15 billion, we can expect human intelligence and technology to comfortably handle the numbers.

Max More, "Life Extension and Overpopulation," www.more.com, 2001.

Faced with these incontestable data on the race between mouths and food, a sophisticated neo-Malthusian would retort that food is only one of many resources upon which people depend. And given our insatiable desire for expanding consumption, mankind's appetite for resources must eventually come into disastrous collision against some limiting natural constraint.

It is impossible today to disprove predictions about tomorrow, but the recent past does not comport with this vision of a world steadily denuded of resources by unchecked population growth and consumerism. Global natural resource constraints have actually been loosening in important areas. That paradox is illustrated by the contrast between global economic production and prices for primary commodities over the twentieth century.

Global Output Exceeds Population Growth

The GDP [gross domestic product] estimates, prepared by eminent economic historian Angus Maddison, cover 56 countries that comprised almost 90 percent of the world's population and over 90 percent of the world's output as of 1992, and thus provide a reasonably close approximation to total global product. The primary commodity price index, developed by the economists Enzo R. Grilli and Maw Cheng Yang, takes the international cost of a market basket of 24 of the most commonly consumed "renewable and non-renewable resources"—foodstuffs, non-food agricultural goods, and metals—and adjusts for inflation. Maddison's estimates extend from 1900 to 1992; Grilli and Yang's, from 1900 to 1986. Both series are authoritative for the trends they depict.

Between 1900 and 1992, by Maddison's reckoning, global output grew at well over twice the pace of population growth, or at almost 3 percent a year. Between 1900 and 1992, this made for a 14-fold increase in the estimated planetary product. That means the global population's demand for goods and services also soared by a factor of 14.

But despite this staggering increase in demand, the relative price of non-fuel primary commodities dropped markedly. Between 1900 and 1986, the cumulative decline in the relative prices of these goods averaged –0.6 percent a year.

This primary commodity index excludes fuels. But adding oil and coal to the primary commodity market basket changes the picture only slightly. One Grilli and Yang series includes those two energy products, weighted to reflect their importance in overall trade. That particular series posts a cumulative decline of over 35 percent between 1900 and 1986, and trends downward at a pace of –0.5 percent per annum for those eight and a half decades.

Looking toward the future, Malthusians imagine that human demands upon a fragile planet are poised to rise indefinitely. Even this assumption may be wrong.

For one thing, patterns of economic activity around the globe have changed radically over the past century. As affluence has increased, the shares of overall output taken by agriculture and manufacturing—which draw heavily upon natural resources—have decreased, while the share accounted for by services has risen correspondingly. The World Bank estimates that services already make up over three-fifths of the world's total economic output. To an ever greater degree, modern economic growth is being driven by the demand for, and consumption of, human knowledge and skills rather than treasures extracted from the earth.

Fertility Levels Are Dropping

Second, it is far from certain that the human population will be growing in the coming millennium. In every industrial democracy in the contemporary world, fertility levels are now below the replacement level; in some of them, far below it. If continued, long-term population declines will result. Indeed, the proportion of humanity living in countries with fertility that will eventually yield population decline is rapidly approaching 50 percent. And for the rest of the world as well, fertility is falling steadily.

Reliable long-term population projections are impossible, since future birth rates are unknowable today. But if the pace of global fertility decline observed over the past 35 years were to continue for another quarter-century, human numbers would peak around the year 2040, and a world depopulation would commence thereafter.

None of this is to suggest that concern with humanity's current and prospective impact on the global environment is unwarranted. Quite the contrary. The case for conservation of, and stewardship over, natural resources is compelling. But responsible conservation and stewardship cannot be promoted by a worldview that strips mankind of its unique dignity, any more than the earth's "carrying capacity" for human beings can be established through rules and parameters derived from populations of fruit flies.

"Another popular misconception is that we can trust in technology to solve our problems."

Science Will Not Solve the Population Problem

Jared Diamond

Jared Diamond argues in the following viewpoint that over-population, environmental problems, and warfare threaten the United States. He asserts that Americans can not depend on science and technology to save them because all current environmental problems are the result of the unanticipated harmful consequences of scientific and technological development. Diamond maintains that current leaders must take action to control population and stop environmental destruction. Jared Diamond is a professor of geography and of environmental health at the University of California, Los Angeles.

As you read, consider the following questions:
1. According to Jared Diamond, when might a society's decline begin?
2. In the author's opinion, what happens to countries that are overpopulated and environmentally stressed?
3. What does the author argue is the secret of societies that acquire good environmental sense?

One of the disturbing facts of history is that so many civilizations collapse. Few people, however, least of all our politicians, realize that a primary cause of the collapse of those societies has been the destruction of the environmental resources on which they depended. Fewer still appreciate that many of those civilizations share a sharp curve of decline. Indeed, a society's demise may begin only a decade or two after it reaches its peak population, wealth, and power.

Recent archaeological discoveries have revealed similar courses of collapse in such otherwise dissimilar ancient societies as the Maya in the Yucatán, the Anasazi in the American Southwest, the Cahokia mound builders outside St. Louis, the Greenland Norse, the statue builders of Easter Island, ancient Mesopotamia in the Fertile Crescent, Great Zimbabwe in Africa, and Angkor Wat in Cambodia. These civilizations, and many others, succumbed to various combinations of environmental degradation and climate change, aggression from enemies taking advantage of their resulting weakness, and declining trade with neighbors who faced their own environmental problems. Because peak population, wealth, resource consumption, and waste production are accompanied by peak environmental impact—approaching the limit at which impact outstrips resources—we can now understand why declines of societies tend to follow swiftly on their peaks.

Importance of a Healthy Environment

These combinations of undermining factors were compounded by cultural attitudes preventing those in power from perceiving or resolving the crisis. That's a familiar problem today. Some of us are inclined to dismiss the importance of a healthy environment, or at least to suggest that it's just one of many problems facing us—an "issue." That dismissal is based on three dangerous misconceptions.

Foremost among these misconceptions is that we must balance the environment against human needs. That reasoning is exactly upside-down. Human needs and a healthy environment are not opposing claims that must be balanced; instead, they are inexorably linked by chains of cause and effect. We need a healthy environment because we need clean water, clean air, wood, and food from the ocean, plus soil and sunlight to grow crops. We need functioning natural ecosystems, with their native species of earthworms, bees, plants, and microbes, to generate and aerate our soils, pollinate our crops, decompose our wastes, and produce our oxygen. We need to prevent toxic substances from accumulating in our water and air and soil. We need to prevent weeds, germs, and other pest species from becoming established in places where they aren't native and where they cause economic damage. Our strongest arguments for a healthy environment are selfish: we want it for ourselves, not for threatened species like snail darters, spotted owls, and Furbish louseworts.

Technology Is Not the Answer

Another popular misconception is that we can trust in technology to solve our problems. Whatever environmental problem you name, you can also name some hoped-for technological solution under discussion. Some of us have faith that we shall solve our dependence on fossil fuels by developing new technologies for hydrogen engines, wind energy, or solar energy. Some of us have faith that we shall solve our food problems with new or soon-to-be-developed genetically modified crops. Some of us have faith that new technologies will succeed in cleaning up the toxic materials in our air, water, soil, and foods without the horrendous cleanup expenses that we now incur.

Those with such faith assume that the new technologies will ultimately succeed, but in fact some of them may succeed and others may not. They assume that the new technologies will succeed quickly enough to make a big difference soon, but all of these major technological changes will actually take five to thirty years to develop and implement—if they catch on at all. Most of all, those with faith assume that new technology won't cause any new problems. In fact, technology merely constitutes increased power, which produces changes that can be either for the better or for the worse. All of our current environmental problems are unanticipated harmful consequences of our existing technology. There is no basis for believing that technology will miraculously stop causing new and unanticipated problems while it

There Is No Technical Solution to Overpopulation

The class of "No technical solution problems" has members. My thesis is that the "population problem," as conventionally conceived, is a member of this class. How it is conventionally conceived needs some comment. It is fair to say that most people who anguish over the population problem are trying to find a way to avoid the evils of overpopulation without relinquishing any of the privileges they now enjoy. They think that farming the seas or developing new strains of wheat will solve the problem—technologically. . . . The solution they seek cannot be found. The population problem cannot be solved in a technical way. . . .

No technical solution can rescue us from the misery of overpopulation. Freedom to breed will bring ruin to all. At the moment, to avoid hard decisions many of us are tempted to propagandize for conscience and responsible parenthood. The temptation must be resisted, because an appeal to independently acting consciences selects for the disappearance of all conscience in the long run, and an increase in anxiety in the short.

The only way we can preserve and nurture other and more precious freedoms is by relinquishing the freedom to breed, and that very soon. "Freedom is the recognition of necessity"—and it is the role of education to reveal to all the necessity of abandoning the freedom to breed.

Garrett Hardin, "Tragedy of the Commons," December 13, 1968.

is solving the problems that it previously produced.

The final misconception holds that environmentalists are fear-mongering, overreacting extremists whose predictions of impending disaster have been proved wrong before and will be proved wrong again. Behold, say the optimists: water still flows from our faucets, the grass is still green, and the supermarkets are full of food. We are more prosperous than ever before, and that's the final proof that our system works.

Population Stress Causes Political Stress

Well, for a few billion of the world's people who are causing us increasing trouble, there isn't any clean water, there is less and less green grass, and there are no supermarkets full of food. . . .

Today, just as in the past, countries that are environmentally stressed, overpopulated, or both are at risk of becoming politically stressed, and of seeing their governments collapse. When people are desperate and undernourished, they blame their government, which they see as responsible for failing to solve their problems. They try to emigrate at any cost. They start civil wars. They kill one another. They figure that they have nothing to lose, so they become terrorists, or they support or tolerate terrorism. . . .

We modern Americans [think we] are fundamentally different from those primitive ancients, and there is nothing that we could learn from them. . . .

We think we are different. In fact, of course, all of those powerful societies of the past thought that they too were unique, right up to the moment of their collapse. It's sobering to consider the swift decline of the ancient Maya, who 1,200 years ago were themselves the most advanced society in the Western Hemisphere, and who, like us now, were then at the apex of their own power and numbers. Two excellent recent books, David Webster's *The Fall of the Ancient Maya* and Richardson Gill's *The Great Maya Droughts*, help bring the trajectory of Maya civilization back to life for us. Their studies illustrate how even sophisticated societies like that of the Maya (and ours) can be undermined by details of rainfall, farming methods, and motives of leaders. . . .

Familiar Strands in the Mayan Collapse

Archaeologists for a long time believed the ancient Maya to be gentle and peaceful people. We now know that Maya warfare was intense, chronic, and unresolvable, because limitations of food supply and transportation made it impossible for any Maya principality to unite the whole region in an empire. The archaeological record shows that wars became more intense and frequent toward the time of the Classic collapse. . . .

We can identify increasingly familiar strands in the Classic Maya collapse. One consisted of population growth outstripping available resources: the dilemma foreseen by Thomas Malthus in 1798. As Webster succinctly puts it in *The Fall of the Ancient Maya*, "Too many farmers grew too many crops on too much of the landscape." While population was increasing, the area of usable farmland paradoxically was decreasing from the effects of deforestation and hillside erosion.

The next strand consisted of increased fighting as more and more people fought over fewer resources. Maya warfare, already endemic, peaked just before the collapse. That is not surprising when one reflects that at least 5 million people, most of them farmers, were crammed into an area smaller than the state of Colorado. That's a high population by the standards of ancient farming societies, even if it wouldn't strike modern Manhattan-dwellers as crowded.

Short-Term Concerns Occupy Leaders

Bringing matters to a head was a drought that, although not the first one the Maya had been through, was the most severe. . . .

The final strand is political. . . . Like most leaders throughout human history, the Maya kings and nobles did not have the leisure to focus on long-term problems, insofar as they perceived them.

What about those same strands today? The United States is also at the peak of its power, and it is also suffering from many environmental problems. Most of us have become aware of more crowding and stress. Most of us living in large American cities are encountering increased commuting delays, because the number of people and hence of cars is increasing faster than the number of freeway lanes. I know plenty of people who in the abstract doubt that the world has a population problem, but almost all of those same people complain to me about crowding, space issues, and traffic experienced in their personal lives. . . .

Not all societies make fatal mistakes. There are parts of the world where societies have unfolded for thousands of years without any collapse, such as Java, Tonga, and (until 1945) Japan. . . . Is there any secret to explain why some societies acquire good environmental sense while others don't? Naturally, part of the answer depends on accidents of individual leaders' wisdom (or lack thereof). But part also depends upon whether a society is organized so as to minimize built-in clashes of interest between its decision-making elites and its masses. . . . A good example of a society that minimizes such clashes of interest is the Netherlands, whose citizens have perhaps the world's highest level of environmental awareness and of membership in environmental organizations. I never understood why, until on a recent trip to the Netherlands I posed the question to three of my Dutch friends while driving through their countryside.

Just look around you, they said. All of this farmland that you see lies below sea level. One fifth of the total area of the Netherlands is below sea level, as much as 22 feet below, because it used to be shallow bays, and we reclaimed it from the sea by surrounding the bays with dikes and then gradually pumping out the water. We call these reclaimed lands "polders." We began draining our polders nearly a thousand years ago. Today, we still have to keep pumping out the water that gradually seeps in. That's what our windmills used to be for, to drive the pumps to pump out the polders. Now we use steam, diesel, and electric pumps instead. In each polder there are lines of them, starting with those farthest from the sea, pumping the water in sequence until the last pump finally deposits it into a river or the ocean. And all of us, rich or poor, live down in the polders. It's not the case that rich people live safely up on top of the dikes while poor people live in the polder bottoms below sea level. If the dikes and pumps fail, we'll all drown together.

Throughout human history, all peoples have been connected to some other peoples, living together in virtual polders. For the ancient Maya, their polder consisted of most of the Yucatán and neighboring areas. When the Classic Maya cities collapsed in the southern Yucatán, refugees may have reached the northern Yucatán, but probably not the Valley of Mexico, and certainly not Florida. Today, our whole world has become one polder, such that events in even Afghanistan and Somalia affect Americans. We do indeed differ from the Maya, but not in ways we might like: we have a much larger population, we have more potent destructive technology, and we face the risk of a worldwide rather than a local decline. Fortunately, we also differ from the Maya in that we know their fate, and they did not. Perhaps we can learn.

Periodical Bibliography

The following articles have been selected to supplement the diverse views presented in this chapter.

Paula Adamick "Baby Talk," *Catholic Insight*, March 2003.

Business Week "How Rich Nations Can Defuse the Population Bomb," May 28, 2001.

Winthrop P. Carty "A Path for Balanced Population Growth?" *Americas* (English edition), March/April 2003.

Tom Flynn "Too Many People," *Free Inquiry*, September 2004.

Daniel M. Fox "Populations and the Law: The Changing Scope of Health Policy," *Journal of Law, Medicine, and Ethics*, Winter 2003.

Frozen Food Digest "More People to Feed," July 2003.

Nick Gillespie "The Census and the Sopranos: Adventures in a Post-Racial America," *Reason*, May 2001.

Lindsey Grant "Optimum Population," *Free Inquiry*, September 2004.

Gene Koretz "Demographic Time Bombs: They Tick for Industrial Nations," *Business Week*, April 21, 2003.

Manufacturing News "Demographics: The United States Is a Population Powerhouse," February 15, 2002.

New Scientist "Teens Rule the World," October 18, 2003.

David Nicholson-Lord "Stop Worrying, Just Interact," *New Statesman*, July 21, 2003.

Don Peck "Population 2050," *Atlantic Monthly*, October 2002.

William Petersen "Age and Sex," *Society*, May 2001.

Kajsa Sundstrom "Can Governments Influence Population Growth?" *OECD Observer*, December 4, 2001.

Sanghan Yea "Are We Prepared for World Population Implosion?" *Futures*, June 2004.

CHAPTER 2

What Problems Are Associated with Population Growth?

Chapter Preface

For years those concerned about population growth have argued that it leads to environmental destruction and hunger. However, according to demographers, ecologists, and hydrologists, of greater concern is the current threat population growth poses to the world's supply of freshwater. The Union of Concerned Scientists and Population Action International jointly report that, "Of all the planet's renewable resources, fresh water may be the most unforgiving. Difficult to purify, expensive to transport, and impossible to substitute, water is essential to food production, to economic development, and to life itself."

Scientists estimate that there is no more freshwater on Earth now than there was two thousand years ago, when the earth's population was less than 3 percent of its current level and significantly less affluent. During the twentieth century alone, the world demand for water increased sixfold, twice the rate of population growth. Author Sandra Postel concludes, "The number of people living in countries experiencing water stress will increase from 467 million in 1995 to over three billion by 2025 as population continues to grow."

Ecologists argue that the increased pollution that inevitably results from population growth further compounds the problem of a limited fresh water supply. Pollution from agriculture, industry, sewage, and increased salinity all degrade water quality. In the United States the loss of wetlands crucial to healthy ecosystems that help regulate water quality is attributed directly to population-caused pollution. The U.S. Fish and Wildlife Service determined that more than half of the country's wetlands were lost in the two hundred years from 1780 to 1980, when the population increased from about 4 million to 257 million.

Population growth stresses the world's freshwater supply by increasing demand for this scarce resource and polluting it. Decreasing fresh water is just one of the problems associated with population growth. Authors in the following chapter debate many others as they explore this important global issue.

"*As population size continues to reach levels never before experienced, and per capita consumption rises, the environment hangs in the balance.*"

Population Growth Is Causing a Global Ecological Disaster

Don Hinrichsen and Bryant Robey

Don Hinrichsen and Bryant Robey argue in the following viewpoint that the growing human population is destroying the earth. They maintain that population increases have caused high levels of deforestation; extinction of plant and animal species; and pollution of oceans, soil, and air. Further, they contend that rich countries such as the United States use the most resources and cause the most pollution. Don Hinrichsen is a senior program officer with the United Nations Population Fund. Bryant Robey is editor of *Population Reports*, published by the Johns Hopkins School of Public Health.

As you read, consider the following questions:
1. According to Hinrichsen and Robey, how many people die from air pollution each year?
2. If humanity does not practice sustainable development, what do the authors predict will happen?
3. Where is almost all population growth currently occurring, in the authors' opinion?

As the [twenty-first] century begins, natural resources are under increasing pressure, threatening public health and development. Water shortages, soil exhaustion, loss of forests, air and water pollution, and degradation of coastlines afflict many areas. As the world's population grows, improving living standards without destroying the environment is a global challenge.

Most developed economies currently consume resources much faster than they can regenerate. Most developing countries with rapid population growth face the urgent need to improve living standards. As we humans exploit nature to meet present needs, are we destroying resources needed for the future?

The Environment Is Getting Worse

In the past decade in every environmental sector, conditions have either failed to improve, or they are worsening:

• *Public health:* Unclean water, along with poor sanitation, kills over 12 million people each year, most in developing countries. Air pollution kills nearly 3 million more. Heavy metals and other contaminants also cause widespread health problems.

• *Food supply:* Will there be enough food to go around? In 64 of 105 developing countries studied by the UN Food and Agriculture Organization, the population has been growing faster than food supplies. Population pressures have degraded some 2 billion hectares of arable land—an area the size of Canada and the U.S.

• *Freshwater:* The supply of freshwater is finite, but demand is soaring as population grows and use per capita rises. By 2025, when world population is projected to be 8 billion, 48 countries containing 3 billion people will face shortages.

• *Coastlines and oceans:* Half of all coastal ecosystems are pressured by high population densities and urban development. A tide of pollution is rising in the world's seas. Ocean fisheries are being overexploited, and fish catches are down.

• *Forests:* Nearly half of the world's original forest cover has been lost, and each year another 16 million hectares are cut, bulldozed, or burned. Forests provide over US$400 billion to the world economy annually and are vital to maintaining healthy ecosystems. Yet, current demand for forest products may exceed the limit of sustainable consumption by 25%.

• *Biodiversity:* The earth's biological diversity is crucial to the continued vitality of agriculture and medicine—and perhaps even to life on earth itself. Yet human activities are pushing many thousands of plant and animal species into extinction. Two of every three species is estimated to be in decline.

• *Global climate change:* The earth's surface is warming due to greenhouse gas emissions, largely from burning fossil fuels. If the global temperature rises as projected, sea levels would rise by several meters, causing widespread flooding. Global warming also could cause droughts and disrupt agriculture.

Toward a Livable Future

How people preserve or abuse the environment could largely determine whether living standards improve or deteriorate. Growing human numbers, urban expansion, and resource exploitation do not bode well for the future. Without practicing sustainable development, humanity faces a deteriorating environment and may even invite ecological disaster.

• *Taking action:* Many steps toward sustainability can be taken today. These include: using energy more efficiently, managing cities better, phasing out subsidies that encourage waste.

• *Stabilizing population:* While population growth has slowed, the absolute number of people continues to increase—by about 1 billion every 13 years. Slowing population growth would help improve living standards and would buy time to protect natural resources. In the long run, to sustain higher living standards, world population size must stabilize.

Population and Sustainable Development

Environmentalists and economists increasingly agree that efforts to protect the environment and to achieve better living standards can be closely linked and are mutually reinforcing. Slowing the increase in population, especially in the face of rising per capita demand for natural resources, can take pressure off the environment and buy time to improve living standards on a sustainable basis.

• As population growth slows, countries can invest more in

Toles. © 1994 by *The Washington Post*. Reproduced by permission of Universal Press Syndicate.

education, health care, job creation, and other improvements that help boost living standards. In turn, as individual income, savings, and investment rise, more resources become available that can boost productivity. This dynamic process has been identified as one of the key reasons that the economies of many Asian countries grew rapidly between 1960 and 1990.

• In recent years fertility has been falling in many developing countries and, as a result, annual world population growth has fallen to about 1.4% in 2000 compared with about 2% in 1960. The UN [United Nations] estimated recently that population is growing by about 78 million per year, down from about 90 million estimated early in the 1990s. Still, at the current pace world population increases by about 1 billion every 13 years. World population surpassed 6 billion in 1999 and is projected to rise to over 8 billion by 2025.

• Globally, fertility has fallen by half since the 1960s, to about three children per woman. In 65 countries, including 9 in the developing world, fertility rates have fallen below replacement level of about two children per woman. Nonetheless, fertility is above replacement level in 123 countries, and in some countries it is substantially above replacement level. In these countries the population continues to increase rapidly. About 1.7 billion people live in 47 countries where the fertility rate averages between three and five children per woman. Another 730 million people live in 44 countries where the average woman has five children or more.

• Almost all population growth is in the developing world. As a result of differences in population growth, Europe's population will decline from 13% to 7% of world population over the next quarter century, while that of sub-Saharan Africa will rise from 10% to 17%. The shares of other regions are projected to remain about the same as today.

• As population and demand for natural resources continue to grow, environmental limits will become increasingly apparent. Water shortages are expected to affect nearly 3 billion people in 2025, with sub-Saharan Africa worst affected. Many countries could avoid environmental crises if they took steps now to conserve and manage supplies and demand better, while slowing population growth by providing families and individuals with information and services needed to make informed choices about reproductive health.

• Family planning programs play a key role. When family planning information and services are widely available and accessible, couples are better able to achieve their fertility desires. "Even in adverse circumstance—low incomes, limited education, and few opportunities for women—family planning programs have meant slower population growth and improved family welfare," the World Bank has noted.

Increasing Population Strains the Environment

If every country made a commitment to population stabilization and resource conservation, the world would be better able to meet the challenges of sustainable development. Practicing sustainable development requires a combination of wise public investment, effective natural resource management, cleaner agricultural and industrial technologies, less pollution, and slower population growth.

Worries about a "population bomb" may have lessened as

fertility rates have fallen, but the world's population is projected to continue expanding until the middle of the century. Just when it stabilizes and thus the level at which it stabilizes will have a powerful effect on living standards and the global environment. As population size continues to reach levels never before experienced, and per capita consumption rises, the environment hangs in the balance.

"The degradation narrative . . . blames poverty on population pressure . . . blames peasants for land degradation . . . and . . . targets migration . . . as an environmental and security threat."

Population Growth Is Unfairly Blamed for Ecological Problems

Betsy Hartmann

Blaming environmental degradation on population increases—especially in developing countries—is misguided, Betsy Hartmann argues in the following viewpoint. Further, Hartmann contends that factions within the United States and international conservation organizations such as the Sierra Club use environmental issues to disguise racist attitudes and policies. Indeed, she argues, these environmentalists blame the fertility of poor people of color for the earth's environmental problems. Betsy Hartmann is the director of the Population and Development Program at Hampshire College in Amherst, Massachusetts.

As you read, consider the following questions:
1. According to Betsy Hartmann, when did the first big greening of hate wave occur in the United States?
2. What message do joint population-environment projects reinforce in poor countries, in the author's opinion?
3. What irony does the author argue is obvious in the American belief in the myth of scarcity?

The greening of hate—blaming environmental degradation on poor populations of color—is once again on the rise, both in the U.S. and overseas. In the U.S., its illogic runs like this: immigrants are the main cause of overpopulation, and overpopulation in turn causes urban sprawl, the destruction of wilderness, pollution, and so forth.

Internationally, it draws on narratives that blame expanding populations of peasants and herders for encroaching on pristine nature.

Immigration Restriction and Coercive Conservation

In the first instance, the main policy 'solution' is immigration restriction; in the second it is coercive conservation, the violent exclusion of local communities from nature preserves. Both varieties of the greening of hate are about policing borders. By stressing the negative role of population growth, both target poor women's fertility as the fundamental root of environmental evil.

In the U.S. the first big greening of hate wave occurred in the mid-1990s when conservative anti-immigrant forces began mobilizing within the Sierra Club, the nation's largest membership-based environmental organization, to pass a ballot initiative supporting a "reduction of net immigration" as a component of a "comprehensive population policy for the United States." An opposing coalition of environmental justice, immigrant rights, and reproductive rights advocates successfully challenged the initiative, and it was voted down in 1998.

Anti-immigrant forces kept on organizing, however. Today, three out of fifteen members of the Sierra Club Board of Directors are key players in the anti-immigrant lobby which is pushing for another ballot initiative in 2005. They are Ben Zuckerman, a UCLA (University of California at Los Angeles) astronomy professor, board member of the Sea Shepherd Conservation Society and a leader of the 1998 ballot initiative; Captain Paul Watson, a founding member of the Greenpeace Foundation and Sea Shepherd; and Doug LaFollette, Wisconsin Secretary of State and board member of Friends of the Earth. All three are conservationists—but what exactly do they want to conserve?

One does not have to scratch very far beneath the surface to find the links between the green wing of the anti-immigration movement and nativism and white supremacy. The summer 2002 issue of the Southern Poverty Law Center's (SPLC) investigative magazine *Intelligence Report* documented these connections, focusing in particular on John Tanton, the main organizer and funder of the anti-immigrant movement, who has close ties to a number of racist hate groups.

The Militarization of Nature Preserves

Ben Zuckerman has described Tanton as "a great environmentalist." Concerned about growing anti-immigration momentum in the Sierra Club, Mark Potok of the SPLC wrote the Club's President in October [2003] warning of "a hostile takeover attempt by forces allied with Tanton and a variety of right-wing extremists." At this point, one of the main right-wing strategies is to get anti-immigration activists to join the Club en masse.

Meanwhile, overseas certain international conservation agencies, notably Conservation International (CI), are greening hate through supporting the militarization of nature preservation. Coercive conservation measures, of course, are nothing new. From colonial times onwards, wildlife conservation efforts have often involved the violent exclusion of local people from their land by game rangers drawn from the ranks of the police, military and prison guards. To legitimize this exclusion, government officials, conservation agencies and aid donors have frequently invoked narratives of expanding human populations destroying pristine landscapes, obscuring the role of resource extraction by state and corporate interests.

Today, one of the most well-known cases of coercive conservation is CI's involvement in the Lacandon Forest in Chiapas, Mexico. In an interview with the *Houston Chronicle*, CI's Chiapas director blamed deforestation there on overpopulation: "It's obvious that the main problem is overpopulation. The children of the farmers don't have any land. They can't all be peasant."

With USAID [United States Agency for International Development] assistance, CI and the World Wildlife Fund are promoting a conservation campaign in the region focused on identifying illegal settlements—often Zapatista communities—which are then forcibly removed by the Mexican army. These efforts are complemented by the government's aggressive female sterilization campaign in the region. CI's close ties to bio-prospecting corporations raise questions of just who the forest is being preserved for.

Joint Population-Environment Projects

Increasingly, international conservation agencies like CI are embarking on what are called "joint population-environment projects" which involve collaborations between family planning and conservation NGOs [nongovernmental agencies]. Despite a professed commitment to communities identifying their own health and environmental needs, the main priority of many such projects is to reduce population growth through increased uptake of contraception. Ideologically, the projects also reinforce the message that it is population growth and the practices of the local people themselves that cause environmental degradation.

Poverty—Not Population—Is the Problem

We must correctly identify what the problem is before we can effectively work to solve it. Environmentalist [Betsy] Hartmann has made a good first diagnosis. Poverty is the problem, not population. . . . Let's hope for the sake of humanity and a thriving natural world that other environmentalists will heed her and turn away from the false, coercive, and possibly racist, population control nostrums still being offered by so many ideological environmentalists.

Ronald Bailey, *Reason*, March 5, 2003.

Population-environment projects often use population monitoring systems, not only to register births, but to track migration. Potentially, such tracking could be of use to defense and intelligence interests, especially in areas of political conflict. A proposed monitoring system for the World Wildlife Fund in the Calakmul Biosphere Reserve in Mexico, where many refugees from Chiapas have settled in recent years, would select key informant households in "sentinel" communities to track immigration. Recruiting households as informants raises disturbing concerns about the impact and intent of such monitoring.

Indeed, coercive conservation provides an important means by which militaries can expand their reach. For example, the U.S. Department of Defense (DOD) now has biodiversity and conservation projects in 15 countries in Africa. In Malawi, for example, it has facilitated the equipping of park guards with semi-automatic weapons. In Central America, the DOD and Southern Command are working to involve national militaries in the MesoAmerican Biological Corridor project, and in the Philippines U.S. environmental aid is a component of current anti-terrorism efforts. Within the U.S., meanwhile, the DOD is now billing itself as the preserver of biodiversity through its 'stewardship' of vast tracks of land it controls for military testing and training. "Biodiversity helps us achieve military readiness in harmony with nature," claims DOD environmental security official Sherri W. Goodman.

The greening of hate has been able to take root in U.S. environmentalism because it draws on widely shared popular beliefs regarding the relationship between population, conservation and the environment. These are the myths of man versus nature, the wilderness ethic, the degradation narrative, and scarcity.

The Man Versus Nature Myth

Man versus nature: Because Americans live in such a rapacious and parochial capitalist society, many assume that people are de facto bad for the environment. There is little understanding of the ways in which human agency can shape the environment in positive ways and even improve biodiversity. There is a big difference, for example, between a corporate corn farm in the Midwest which uses massive applications of pesticides and a peasant corn plot in Mexico where new seed varieties are constantly evolving over time and other species of plants and animals can thrive in the non-polluted environment.

Similarly, there is a big difference between a city with a strong zoning department, environmental regulations and a well-developed public transport system and one in which business prerogatives and an unregulated real estate market shape development and encourage urban sprawl. Political and technological choices, not levels of immigration, explain the difference between the ecologically healthy city and the unhealthy one.

The man vs. nature myth is rooted in a problematic tradition of conservation biology which views human populations as behaving in the same way as exponentially growing pondweed or bacteria in a petri dish. In the U.S. major environmental figures like Paul Ehrlich of population bomb fame and Garrett Hardin, who advocates pushing the poor off the lifeboat, come from this tradition. It not only ignores the capacity of humans for rational thought and action, but history, politics, economics, and demography.

It is a particularly insidious ideological trap because it leads to an acceptance of wars and diseases like AIDS as 'natural' checks on human population growth. The website of the anti-immigrant group, Support a Comprehensive Sierra Club Population Policy (SUSPS), currently features two stories about "My Bacteria Neighbors" and the "Lily Pond Parable." Use your imagination to fill in the blanks.

The Wilderness Ethic

The Wilderness Ethic: William Cronin has described the unique place the idea of wilderness holds in the American psyche, both as a romantic, sublime, quasi-religious force and a vehicle for frontier nostalgia. The ways in which wilderness is constructed have a number of problematic outcomes. The ahistorical myth of wilderness as "virgin" land obscures the systematic forced migration and genocide of its original Native American inhabitants.

By locating nature in the far-off wild, it allows people to evade responsibility for environmental protection closer to their homes. And it is geographically parochial, blinding many Americans to the complex ways in which people relate to the land in other countries and cultures. Critiquing the wilderness ethic does not mean one is opposed to national parks and nature protection—rather, it calls for equitable and democratic processes to ensure local communities are not pushed off their lands and robbed of their livelihoods.

The Degradation Narrative

The degradation narrative: This is the belief that population pressure-induced poverty makes Third World peasants degrade their environments by over-farming marginal lands. The ensuing soil depletion and desertification then lead them to migrate elsewhere as "environmental refugees," either to ecologically vulnerable rural areas where the vicious cycle is once again set in motion or to cities where they become a primary source of political instability.

The degradation narrative has proved particularly popular in Western policy circles because it kills a number of birds with one stone: it blames poverty on population pressure, and not, for example, on lack of land reform or off-farm employment opportunities; it blames peasants for land degradation, obscuring the role of commercial agriculture and extractive industries; and it targets migration both as an environmental and security threat. It is a way of homogenizing all rural people in the Global South into one big destructive force, reinforcing simplistic Us vs. Them, West vs. the Rest dichotomies.

Last but not least is the myth of scarcity—the belief, common in the U.S., that there are not enough resources to go around and the human population is close to overshooting the carrying capacity of the earth. There is a certain irony in the fact that the country with the most profligate waste and consumption levels is the most obsessed with planetary resource limits (and the least willing to do anything about them).

Andrew Ross makes the point that fears about scarcities of natural resources parallel the manufacturing of social scarcities by competitive capitalist regimes. In the public consciousness, imposed limits to growth in social welfare expenditures become intertwined with the notion of environmental limits. Missing from the picture, of course, is the role of the rich in gobbling up both economic and natural resources at an ever-expanding rate, undermining effective environmental protection, and refusing to invest in new, non-polluting energy sources.

Challenging these myths is no easy matter, but challenge them we must if we are going to effectively resist the greening of hate and the conservation of racism.

"Rising demand, through population growth and increasing affluence, is outpacing [food] production."

Overpopulation Contributes to World Hunger

Geoffrey Lean

In the following viewpoint Geoffrey Lean claims that global food production is inadequate for the growing population and that world reserves of foodstuffs are rapidly dwindling. He blames harvest decreases on loss of fertile land due to population growth and overcultivation. Lean argues further that increasing affluence, which encourages people to eat more meat rather than depending on grains, also decreases land available for cultivation. He insists that slowing population growth by international funding of contraception and health-care programs for women is the best solution to world hunger. Geoffrey Lean is the environment editor of the *Independent*, a British daily newspaper.

As you read, consider the following questions:

1. According to Geoffrey Lean, for how many years has the world's harvest of food fallen short?
2. On average, how many children does each woman in the world now bear, according to the author?
3. What does the author argue is the reason that the Bush administration has cut contributions to the UN Population Fund?

The world is consistently failing to grow enough crops to feed itself, alarming official statistics show. Humanity has squeaked through so far by eating its way into stockpiles built up in better times. But these have fallen sharply and are now at the lowest level on record.

The UN's [United Nation's] Food and Agriculture Organisation's (FAO) latest report on global food production says that this year's [2004] harvest is expected to fall short of meeting consumption for the fifth year running. Even a forecast record harvest this year is failing to ease the crisis. This suggests that rising demand, through population growth and increasing affluence, is outpacing production, fulfilling the gloomy predictions of Thomas Malthus over 200 years ago.

Scarcity of Energy and Water

Warnings of increasing scarcity of two other key resources came last week [August 2004]. Mark Clare, the managing director of *British Gas*, said: "The era of cheap energy is over." And experts at an international symposium in Stockholm foretold an imminent world crisis as underground reserves of water are increasingly pumped dry. A major UN-backed conference in London this week will attempt to revive a global effort to tackle population growth. Countdown 2015 will assess an international plan of action agreed 10 years ago and make recommendations for the next decade.

Between 1950 and 1997 the world's grain harvest almost trebled to around 1,900 million tons. But then production effectively stagnated: since 1999 it has fallen behind consumption very year. The FAO report—the latest edition of its quarterly review, *Food Outlook*—predicts "a substantial increase" in the harvest, to 1,956 million tons, by far the biggest ever. But it warns that even this level of output would not keep pace with consumption, causing "a fifth consecutive drawdown of global cereal stocks."

Experts say that recent good weather in almost all the main growing regions, in contrast to Britain where August rain has devastated crops, has boosted the bumper harvest even further. But even optimistic estimates do not expect any recovery of stocks—now at their lowest level ever, well below the 70 days' supply needed for world food security. Lester

Brown, president of Washington's Earth Policy Institute, says: "There has been the odd bad year or two in the past. But this is the first time in history that we have had such an extended period where the world has failed to feed itself.

Millions Die from Hunger

Millions of children in poor countries will die of hunger in the next few years. If there are more children than can be adequately fed, cared for and educated, the balance will be forced into slavery, prostitution, crime and the war machinery. Religions have continuously missed their chance to improve the fate of children. Some say there is enough food available and that it is only a question of distribution. This view is another example of approaching the problem by its secondary cause. It will work only until all available land resources—including all rain forests—are gone. By then the population will have grown to proportions that cause worldwide catastrophic hunger. It will then be too late, even for an all-out population reduction. Only strict and worldwide population control can solve this problem in the long run. The ratio of births to deaths must be reduced to below 1 until a sustainable number of people is attained (estimated by some researchers as about 2.5 billion for the world).

Felix Voirol, www.philosophy.ch/ecology/crisese.htm, 2002.

"This year's harvest is going to be extraordinarily good. It is striking that even in such an exceptional year we are unable to rebuild stocks." The situation is particularly serious in China, where the grain harvest has fallen in four of the past five years. In 2003 it grew 70 million tons less than in 1998—a drop that is equivalent to the entire production of Canada, a leading grain exporter.

Population Growth and Loss of Land

Before 1999 China built up large stocks but has since eaten its way through half of them. Experts say that if the giant country has to start importing grain, its massive needs will increase scarcity and drive up food prices worldwide. China's harvests have partly fallen because it is rapidly losing fertile land as cities spread and soil erodes through overcultivation—and because the groundwater needed to irrigate crops is drying up.

It is the same story worldwide. Population growth and the loss of land have cut the amount of fertile land available to feed each person in half since 1960. And more than half the world's people live in countries where water tables are falling rapidly and wells are running dry. Experts at the Stockholm Water Symposium [in August 2004] warned that millions of wells throughout Asia were rapidly depleting supplies; the amount of irrigated land in the Indian state of Tamil Nadu, for example, has shrunk by half in the last decade.

Rising affluence is partly responsible. As people become better off they eat more meat: animals consume several pounds of grain for every pound of meat they produce. But population growth is even more significant. This week's conference, partly organised by the London-based International Planned Parenthood Federation and Ted Turner's United Nations Foundation, marks a particularly important staging post in the world's attempts to tackle overpopulation.

The meeting can celebrate considerable success. The rate of increase in human numbers has slowed dramatically—from 2 per cent a year in 1970 to 1.3 per cent now. Forty years ago, on average, every woman in the world bore six children: now that figure is below three. The doom-mongering predictions of the 1970s—that, for example, the population could grow to 60 billion, nearly 10 times the present level—have long been abandoned.

Population Crisis Continues

But there is still a crisis: 76 million people are born each year—about 240,000 a day—adding to the demand for food, water and other resources. The UN does not expect world population to stabilise until it has risen from today's 6.4 billion to 9 billion. Nearly half of the world's people are under 25, and mostly able to reproduce. And the greatest growth is expected in the countries least able to cope with it: the UN estimates that the population of the world's 48 poorest countries could treble by 2050.

Ten years ago 179 countries agreed on a practical plan of action at the International Conference on Population and Development in Cairo. It included increasing the availability of contraceptives but also other measures that have a dramatic effect on population growth, especially improving the lives of young women through providing schooling and healthcare. This has shown results, but the world has provided less than half the funds needed to implement it. And the programme is now being sabotaged by the Bush administration, which has cut off its contributions to the UN Population Fund and crippled national programmes because of its opposition to abortion.

"According to the United Nations' figures, since World War II, world food production per person has increased by 30%."

Overpopulation Is Not the Main Cause of World Hunger

Pregnant Pause

Overpopulation is not the cause of world hunger, editors from Pregnant Pause argue in the following viewpoint. Indeed, they claim, yearly food production increases more than meet the needs of the world's growing population. They maintain that the increasing number of farmers working the land plus the use of irrigation, fertilizer, and selective breeding to improve crops have helped food production outpace population growth. They also insist that there is plenty of tillable land available to grow crops—less than one-third is currently under production. Pregnant Pause is a pro-life organization located in Fairborn, Ohio.

As you read, consider the following questions:

1. In the authors' opinion, what part of Thomas Malthus's theory of population was wrong?
2. What does UNICEF claim could prevent the majority of childhood deaths in developing countries?
3. According to the authors, how much has food production per person increased in developing countries?

Population control activists routinely argue that the world cannot continue to support an ever-increasing population. Resources are finite, and they are starting to run out, or will run out soon.

Perhaps the most important resource is food. The consequences of running out of food are surely more dire than running out of almost any other resource. So let's take a look at the present state and future prospects of the world's food supply.

Malthus Was Wrong

Thomas Malthus wrote one of the first books advocating population control, in 1798. It bore the catchy title, *An Essay on the Principle of Population as It Affects the Future of Society*. He analyzed the situation as follows: Population growth is dependent on the current population—the more people there are at any given time, the more children will be born, and the population will grow faster and faster every year. This is called "exponential growth". But food production is limited by available land, water for irrigation, and so on. These things are finite. At best food production might increase by the same amount every year. This is called "arithmetic growth". But eventually even that rate of growth will be impossible to maintain, as available land, water, and so on are used up, and increases in food production must start to taper off. Thus, with the number of people growing faster and faster, and food production growing slower and slower, sooner or later it will simply be impossible to feed all the people, and there will be mass starvation.

In Malthus' time the population of Britain was about 11 million, which he considered the country was just barely able to feed. He wrote that the idea that the nation could feed double this number, or 22 million, was "probably a greater increase than could with reason be expected". To support double this again, or 44 million, would be "impossible to suppose", and that this impossibility "must be evident to those who have the slightest acquantance with agricultural subjects". Britain today has a population of 58 million, who do not appear to be starving.

What was wrong with Malthus' analysis? He was essentially correct about population growth: it does indeed tend to increase exponentially. But he was completely wrong about food production. The following chart shows what Malthus expected to happen to food production, and what has actually happened. I use wheat as the example because it is a basic food eaten by people all over the world, and statistics on world production are readily available.

Food Production Increases

The line labelled "Malthus" shows food production as Malthus predicted it would be: starting out as a straight-line increase and gradually tapering off. The line labelled "Actual" shows food production as it actually was: increasing at a faster and faster pace.

World Wheat Production

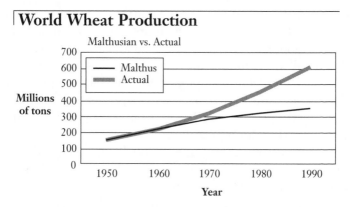

Pregnant Pause, www.pregnantpause.org, September 10, 2000.

Population control advocates today admit that Malthus was overly pessismistic, but they still hold to his basic ideas. They continue to warn that the disaster is almost upon us. Occasionally some will even say that it is already beginning. For example, Paul Ehrlich, one of the leading population control advocates, recently wrote that "40,000 children die daily from hunger-related diseases". This comes to 14.6 million per year. It's not clear where he gets this number from, as no one is keeping such statistics on a global basis. Presumably most of these starvation deaths must be occurring in the developing world—few people in the US or Europe are dying of starvation. But according to UNICEF [United Nations Children's Fund], about 12.9 million children in the developing world die each year, of all causes combined. Of these, UNICEF claims that 8.1 million could be prevented with proper medical care, primarily vaccines.

But as the population grows there is less and less food to go around, right? Well, let's see. The following chart shows world food production per person since 1950, based on the United Nations computation of the total of all types of food.

The Green Revolution

Hmm. According to the United Nations' figures, since World War II, world food production per person has increased by 30%. Note we are not saying that food production has increased by 30%, but food production *per person*. And even this incredible increase is surely less than what could be done. For the overwhelming majority of Americans and Europeans, the problem is not that they have too little to eat, but that they eat too much. So there is no need for food production for these people to increase. If we just look at the developing countries, where some people may really need more food, production has increased 38%.

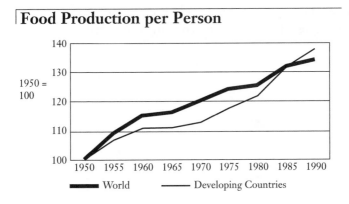

Food Production per Person

United Nations State of Food and Agriculture reports.

How is it possible to continue to increase production year after year like this? For most of history, and even today in many parts of the world, the major limit on food production is the number of farmers available to work the land. As the population grows, so does the number of farmers. In addition, what's really enabled the increase of the last few decades has been the so-called "Green Revolution": irrigation, selective breeding of improved crops, and fertilizer. When I was originally researching this topic I happened to come across a list of the leading exporters of various food-stuffs. One showed the top ten wheat exporters. I could have guessed most of them: the US, France, Canada, Australia, etc. But #10 was quite a surprise: Saudi Arabia. That's really a place you think of as lush farmland, isn't it? They now export over $200 million worth of wheat each year.

Some argue that these advances have now reached their limits, that all that was accomplished was postponing the disaster, and that we are now once again pushing the limits. Well, it would surely be pessimistic to assume that after decades of advances, agricultural technology is now going to stop dead. But even if it did, we could just plant more crops. The UN came out with a study back in 1970, which is a little out-of-date but there is no reason to believe things have changed much since then, on how much land in the world is suitable for agriculture. If you assume that we are not going to cut down any forests or make other major changes to the landscape, there are about 4.4 billion hectares. Of this, 1.4 billion, or less than a third, are actually being used to grow crops.

*"The explosion of human population . . .
coupled with the unequal distribution and
consumption of wealth . . . is the
underlying cause of the Sixth Extinction."*

Overpopulation Could Lead to Humanity's Extinction

Niles Eldredge

While the five previous global biotic turnovers—extinctions—were caused by physical phenomena such as climate change, the sixth extinction currently under way is caused by changes brought about by the earth's huge human population, Niles Eldredge argues in the following viewpoint. He maintains that human overpopulation is the direct cause of ecosystem stress and species extinction in the modern world. Further, Eldredge insists that unless human population numbers and consumption patterns stabilize, human beings will become extinct. Niles Eldredge is the curator in chief of the Hall of Diversity exhibit at the American Museum of Natural History in New York.

As you read, consider the following questions:

1. According to Niles Eldredge, how many species is the earth losing per year?
2. What two arguments does the author offer to prove that native species typically became extinct when modern humans arrived?
3. In the author's opinion, what is the single most profound ecological change in the entire history of life?

There is little doubt left in the minds of professional biologists that Earth is currently faced with a mounting loss of species that threatens to rival the five great mass extinctions of the geological past. As long ago as 1993, Harvard biologist E.O. Wilson estimated that Earth is currently losing something on the order of 30,000 species per year—which breaks down to the even more daunting statistic of some three species per hour. Some biologists have begun to feel that this biodiversity crisis—this "Sixth Extinction"—is even more severe, and more imminent, than Wilson had supposed.

Extinction in the Past

The major global biotic turnovers were all caused by physical events that lay outside the normal climatic and other physical disturbances which species, and entire ecosystems, experience and survive. What caused them?

• *First major extinction (c. 440 million years ago):* Climate change (relatively severe and sudden global cooling) seems to have been at work at the Ordovician mass extinction that caused such pronounced change in marine life (little or no life existed on land at that time). 25% of families lost (a family may consist of a few to thousands of species).

• *Second major extinction (c. 370 million years ago):* The next such event, near the end of the Devonian Period, may or may not have been the result of global climate change. 19% of families lost.

• *Third major extinction (c. 245 million years ago):* Scenarios explaining what happened at the greatest mass extinction event of them all (so far, at least!) at the end of the Permian Period have been complex amalgams of climate change perhaps rooted in plate tectonics movements. Very recently, however, evidence suggests that a bolide impact similar to the end-Cretaceous event may have been the cause. 54% of families lost.

• *Fourth major extinction (c. 210 million years ago):* The event at the end of the Triassic Period, shortly after dinosaurs and mammals had first evolved, also remains difficult to pin down in terms of precise causes. 23% of families lost.

• *Fifth major extinction (c. 65 million years ago):* Most famous, perhaps, was the most recent of these events at the end-Cretaceous. It wiped out the remaining terrestrial dinosaurs and marine ammonites, as well as many other species across the phylogenetic spectrum, in all habitats sampled from the fossil record. Consensus has emerged in the past decade that this event was caused by one (possibly multiple) collisions between Earth and an extraterrestrial bolide (probably cometary). Some geologists, however, point to the great volcanic event that produced the Deccan traps of India as part of the chain of physical events that disrupted ecosystems so severely that many species on land and sea rapidly succumbed to extinction. 17% of families lost.

The Sixth Extinction Is Different from Previous Events

At first glance, the physically caused extinction events of the past might seem to have little or nothing to tell us about the current Sixth Extinction, which is a patently human-caused event. For there is little doubt that humans are the direct cause of ecosystem stress and species destruction in the modern world through such activities as:

- transformation of the landscape
- overexploitation of species
- pollution
- the introduction of alien species

And because *Homo sapiens* is clearly a species of animal (however behaviorally and ecologically peculiar an animal), the Sixth Extinction would seem to be the first recorded global extinction event that has a biotic, rather than a physical, cause.

Yet, upon further reflection, human impact on the planet is a direct analogue of the Cretaceous cometary collision. Sixty-five million years ago that extraterrestrial impact—through its sheer explosive power, followed immediately by its injections of so much debris into the upper reaches of the atmosphere that global temperatures plummeted and, most critically, photosynthesis was severely inhibited—wreaked havoc on the living systems of Earth. That is precisely what human beings are doing to the planet right now: humans are causing vast physical changes on the planet.

We can divide the Sixth Extinction into two discrete phases:

- Phase One began when the first modern humans began to disperse to different parts of the world about 100,000 years ago.
- Phase Two began about 10,000 years ago when humans turned to agriculture.

The Beginning of Human Migration

The first phase began shortly after *Homo sapiens* evolved in Africa and the anatomically modern humans began migrating out of Africa and spreading throughout the world. Humans reached the Middle East 90,000 years ago. They were in Europe starting around 40,000 years ago. Neanderthals, who had long lived in Europe, survived our arrival for less than 10,000 years, but then abruptly disappeared—victims, according to many paleoanthropologists, of our arrival through outright warfare or the more subtle, though potentially no less devastating effects, of being on the losing side of ecological competition.

A Period of Mass Extinction

There is virtual unanimity among scientists that we have entered a period of mass extinction not seen since the age of the dinosaurs, an emerging global crisis that could have disastrous effects on our future food supplies, our search for new medicines, and on the water we drink and the air we breathe. Estimates vary, but extinction is figured by experts to be taking place between 100 to 1,000 times higher than natural "background" extinction.

Gary Strieker, www.cnn.com, August 23, 2002.

Everywhere, shortly after modern humans arrived, many (especially, though by no means exclusively, the larger) native species typically became extinct. Humans were like bulls in a China shop:

- They disrupted ecosystems by overhunting game species, which never experienced contact with humans before.
- And perhaps they spread microbial disease-causing organisms as well.

The fossil record attests to human destruction of ecosystems:

• Humans arrived in large numbers in North America roughly 12,500 years ago—and sites revealing the butchering of mammoths, mastodons and extinct buffalo are well documented throughout the continent. The demise of the bulk of the La Brea tar pit Pleistocene fauna coincided with our arrival.

• The Caribbean lost several of its larger species when humans arrived some 8000 years ago.

• Extinction struck elements of the Australian megafauna much earlier—when humans arrived some 40,000 years ago. Madagascar—something of an anomaly, as humans only arrived there two thousand years ago—also fits the pattern well: the larger species (elephant birds, a species of hippo, plus larger lemurs) rapidly disappeared soon after humans arrived.

Indeed only in places where earlier hominid species had lived (Africa, of course, but also most of Europe and Asia) did the fauna, already adapted to hominid presence, survive the first wave of the Sixth Extinction pretty much intact. The rest of the world's species, which had never before encountered hominids in their local ecosystems, were as naively unwary as all but the most recently arrived species (such as Vermilion Flycatchers) of the Galapagos Islands remain to this day.

The Sixth Extinction Is Continuing

Phase two of the Sixth Extinction began around 10,000 years ago with the invention of agriculture—perhaps first in the Natufian culture of the Middle East. Agriculture appears to have been invented several different times in various different places, and has, in the intervening years, spread around the entire globe.

Agriculture represents the single most profound ecological change in the entire 3.5 billion-year history of life. With its invention:

• humans did not have to interact with other species for survival, and so could manipulate other species for their own use

• humans did not have to adhere to the ecosystem's carrying capacity, and so could overpopulate

Homo sapiens became the first species to stop living inside local ecosystems. All other species, including our ancestral hominid ancestors, all pre-agricultural humans, and remnant hunter-gatherer societies still extant exist as semi-isolated populations playing specific roles (i.e., have "niches") in local ecosystems. This is not so with post-agricultural revolution humans, who in effect have stepped outside local ecosystems. Indeed, to develop agriculture is essentially to declare war on ecosystems—converting land to produce one or two food crops, with all other native plant species all now classified as unwanted "weeds"—and all but a few domesticated species of animals now considered as pests.

The total number of organisms within a species is limited by many factors—most crucial of which is the "carrying capacity" of the local ecosystem: given the energetic needs and energy-procuring adaptations of a given species, there are only so many squirrels, oak trees and hawks that can inhabit a given stretch of habitat. Agriculture had the effect of removing the natural local-ecosystem upper limit of the size of human populations. Though crops still fail regularly, and famine and disease still stalk the land, there is no doubt that agriculture in the main has had an enormous impact on human population size:

• Estimates vary, but range between 1 and 10 million people on earth 10,000 years ago.

• There are now over 6 billion people.

• The numbers continue to increase logarithmically—so that there will be 8 billion by 2020.

• There is presumably an upper limit to the carrying capacity of humans on earth—of the numbers that agriculture can support—and that number is usually estimated at between 13–15 billion, though some people think the ultimate numbers might be much higher.

People: The Cause of the Sixth Extinction

This explosion of human population, especially in the post–Industrial Revolution years of the past two centuries, coupled with the unequal distribution and consumption of wealth on the planet, is the underlying cause of the Sixth Extinction. There is a vicious cycle:

• More lands are cleared and more efficient production

techniques (most recently engendered largely through genetic engineering) to feed the growing number of humans—and in response, the human population continues to expand.

• Higher fossil energy use is helping agriculture spread, further modifying the environment.

• Humans continue to fish (12 of the 13 major fisheries on the planet are now considered severely depleted) and harvest timber for building materials and just plain fuel, pollution, and soil erosion from agriculture creates dead zones in fisheries (as in the Gulf of Mexico).

• While the human Diaspora has meant the spread, as well, of alien species that more often than not thrive at the detriment of native species. For example, invasive species have contributed to 42% of all threatened and endangered species in the U.S.

Stopping the Sixth Extinction

The world's ecosystems have been plunged into chaos, with some conservation biologists thinking that no system, not even the vast oceans, remains untouched by human presence. Conservation measures, sustainable development, and, ultimately, stabilization of human population numbers and consumption patterns seem to offer some hope that the Sixth Extinction will not develop to the extent of the third global extinction, some 245 million years ago, when 90% of the world's species were lost.

Though it is true that life, so incredibly resilient, has always recovered (though after long lags) after major extinction spasms, it is only after whatever has caused the extinction event has dissipated. That cause, in the case of the Sixth Extinction, is ourselves—*Homo sapiens.* This means we can continue on the path to our own extinction, or, preferably, we modify our behavior toward the global ecosystem of which we are still very much a part. The latter must happen before the Sixth Extinction can be declared over, and life can once again rebound.

"Whatever happens now, the world's population is primed to start diminishing for probably the first time since the Black Death in the 14th century."

Declining Population Is a Serious Problem

Fred Pearce

In the following viewpoint Fred Pearce argues that a declining, aging population will cause serious social and economic problems for the world in the decades to come. He maintains that fertility rates around the world have declined as many women realize that it is too difficult to have children and a career, and have chosen not to have children. Pearce contends that the burden of an aging population combined with the lack of a young workforce will result in harmful social and political change. Fred Pearce is a professor of biological chemistry at University College London and a frequent contributor to *New Scientist*.

As you read, consider the following questions:
1. According to the author, how much did the world's population increase during the twentieth century?
2. In Pearce's opinion, what is the single common factor uniting nations with fast-falling fertility rates?
3. Which country is poised to become the first African nation with a declining population, in the author's opinion?

Fred Pearce, "Mamma Mia: Italian Women Are Terrifying Demographers," *New Scientist*, vol. 175, July 20, 2002, pp. 38–41. Copyright © 2002 by Reed Elsevier Business Publishing, Ltd. Reproduced by permission.

The baby boom seems to be turning to baby bust. Not just in the rich world but increasingly in poor countries too. Within 50 years, the world's population could be in free fall. And the only way out could be for men to behave more like women.

To see the future in its starkest form, take a look at Italy, where Isabella, Clara and Bianca are less likely to be making babies than young women anywhere else in Europe. With splendid irony, the country that is home to the Catholic Church, noted for its opposition to artificial birth control, is notching up super-low fertility rates way below replacement levels. At just 1.2 children born to each Italian woman, the rate is little more than half the figure needed to prevent the population plummeting. It's a similar picture, if a little less extreme, the world over.

Declining Population Means an Older World

A future decline in the world's population sounds like a good thing. Certainly, it will reduce the pressures on global natural resources. But a world of falling population will be very different from the one we know now: a much older world, and perhaps a less innovative, more conservative one. It will be a world in which labour is in increasingly short supply and the richest countries compete for immigrants who can supply it, not turn them away.

And the relationship between the sexes will become a fundamental political issue, as countries seek to revive their child-bearing resources. Indeed, to stave off the spectre of demographic decline, some countries may become willing to take ever more radical, even draconian measures, with major implications for the personal liberties of us all.

It's quite a turnaround. Ever since the 1970s, forecasters have been scaring us with population figures which appear to wildly outstrip even the most optimistic projections for resources such as food, water and land, while triggering runaway global warming and an even more polluted and paved planet.

And so far, the figures have borne them out. During the 20th century, the world's population increased almost fourfold, from 1.6 to 6 billion. The baby boom, which peaked in mid-century, has not yet ended. But in the background, fertility has been falling fast. In 1950, worldwide the average woman had five children. Today she has just 2.7, and the continued collapse of fertility is set to become the dominant demographic feature of the 21st century.

Demographers have assumed that during this century most of the world's women would settle down in a conventional Western-style nuclear family with mother, father and two children. That would ensure a stable world population by 2100 of perhaps of 10 billion. But nobody told women about the plan, and there is a growing notion that Italy is leading the way to a future of fertility rates far lower than replacement levels.

Fertility Rates Declining

The rule of thumb is that "replacement" fertility requires 2.1 children per woman; the extra 0.1 compensates for girls who do not live long enough to have families. At 1.2 babies per woman, Italy is clearly falling a long way short. But it's not alone. Its southern European neighbours, Spain and Greece, have similar fertility rates, as do the Czech Republic and former Soviet states such as Russia and Armenia. The amazing bottom line is that new UN [United Nations] population forecasts, to be finalised later this year [2002], are expected to conclude that within two generations four out of five of the world's women will be having two children or fewer.

So why is the world still oblivious to this coming demographic shift? It's largely because the children of the greatest population explosion in the planet's history are now of childbearing age. Even with their much-reduced fertility rates, they are bringing many more babies into the world than ever before. This, combined with rising life expectancy, is keeping Europe's population stable, and boosting that of the world as a whole by around 80 million a year. But by the time the 20th-century baby boomers start to die off and the tide turns, it will be hard to halt a population crash. Almost whatever happens now, the world's population is primed to start diminishing for probably the first time since the Black Death [bubonic plague] in the 14th century.

The key questions are why women are choosing to have

Population Growth Is Falling

A [close] look at demographic trends shows that the rate of world population growth has fallen by more than 40 percent since the late 1960s. And forecasts by the UN [United Nations] and other organizations show that even in the absence of major wars or pandemics, the number of human beings on the planet could well start to decline within the lifetime of today's children. Demographers at the International Institute for Applied Systems Analysis predict that human population will peak (at 9 billion) by 2070 and then start to contract. Long before then, many nations will shrink in absolute size, and the average age of the world's citizens will shoot up dramatically. Moreover, the populations that will age fastest are in the Middle East and other underdeveloped regions. During the remainder of this century, even sub-Saharan Africa will likely grow older than Europe is today.

The root cause of these trends is falling birthrates. Today, the average woman in the world bears half as many children as did her counterpart in 1972. No industrialized country still produces enough children to sustain its population over time, or to prevent rapid population aging. Germany could easily lose the equivalent of the current population of what was once East Germany over the next half-century. Russia's population is already contracting by three-quarters of a million a year. Japan's population, meanwhile, is expected to peak as early as 2005, and then to fall by as much as one-third over the next 50 years—a decline equivalent, the demographer Hideo Ibe has noted, to that experienced in medieval Europe during the plague.

Although many factors are at work, the changing economics of family life is the prime factor in discouraging childbearing. In nations rich and poor, under all forms of government, as more and more of the world's population moves to urban areas in which children offer little or no economic reward to their parents, and as women acquire economic opportunities and reproductive control, the social and financial costs of childbearing continue to rise.

Phillip Longman, *Foreign Affairs*, May/June 2004.

fewer offspring, and how far their increasing reluctance to take up motherhood will go. Most obviously, the declining death rate, particularly among children, due to better health and medical services, has meant people don't feel they need to have so many children. Other factors have accelerated the process. Urbanisation is certainly one. On a farm, even young children are an asset, minding the animals and helping with the harvest. In cities it's a different story: kids are more likely to be a liability—in purely economic terms, at least. When they are young, they need looking after full-time, and when they are older they need educating to get any sort of job.

On top of that, cultural changes have increasingly liberated women from the home and child-rearing. In poor countries with a traditional patriarchal society, the spread of TV has opened many women's eyes to a whole new world, and modern birth control methods have allowed them to turn those aspirations into reality. "Getting married and having children are simply not as important as they used to be," says Tim Dyson of the London School of Economics.

No Forced Contraception

Today, more than 60 countries have fertility rates below replacement levels. None shows any sign of sustained recovery. The club now encompasses much of the Caribbean, Japan, Korea and China, the world's most populous nation. This year Thailand, Sri Lanka and Iran are likely to join. Mindful of the "enormous implications" for the future of our species, the UN population division's director Joseph Charmie called a conference of experts in New York in March this year to analyse the phenomenon. A succession of scientists from large countries that have helped drive global population growth in the past half-century told the conference that they expected their own national fertility rates to fall below replacement levels within 20 years. They included India, Brazil, Indonesia, Mexico and Turkey.

Few of these countries, bar China, have forced contraception on their populations. Rather the reverse. Opposition from the Catholic Church has ensured that Brazil has no state family planning programme. Even so, millions of its women have attended sterilisation clinics, and fertility has halved in 20 years to today's 2.3.

The case of Iran is even more remarkable. In 1994, the mullahs ruling the country went to a UN population conference in Cairo and declared opposition to much of the international agenda for cutting birth rates. But back home, women were taking charge of their bodies and sending fertility rates crashing from 5.5 children per woman in 1988 to just 2.2 in 2000.

Prosperity is no longer a necessary passport to reducing national fertility. Bangladesh remains among the half-dozen poorest nations outside Africa. Its girls are among the least educated and marry younger than most. Yet they give birth to just 3.3 children, half the number their mothers had. In Vietnam, which is poorer still, women halved their fertility to 2.3 children in the decade to the mid-1990s.

Rich or poor, socialist or capitalist, Muslim or Catholic, with tough family planning policies or none, most countries tell the same story: women are voting with their wombs. Two major studies have recently failed to find any common factors uniting nations with fast-falling fertility, other than availability of affordable contraception.

A Statement of Modernity

Dyson is among the demographers who have a new theory for what is happening, "cultural diffusion." Not having children has become a statement of modernity and emancipation, and women are unlikely to give up the new freedoms. They are also taking over from their brothers and husbands the role of shaping their societies. "Go to rural India," says Dyson, "and you find that women are fed up with the men, who seem to be going nowhere. It is the women who are running the farms. It is the women who are getting jobs and taking charge. They don't have time to have children any more." With men no longer in charge, their usefulness to society and the old Indian preference for sons may diminish as a result, he says. That, too, will help reduce fertility as couples see daughters as well as sons as potential heads of a new generation.

Where is this all leading? Jack Caldwell of the Australian National University in Canberra, doyen of demographers, is among those convinced that "Italy is the future." Its super-low fertility arises from female emancipation, or rather from its faltering progress, he says. Isabella and her friends are educated as well as or better than their suitors. They have prospects. The last thing they want is to be like their mothers, stuck at home rearing children.

French demographer Jean-Claude Chesnais of the National Institute for Demographic Studies in Paris goes further. With poor state childcare provision, and most men unlikely to help in looking after their offspring, "the obstacles to childbearing in countries like Italy are enormous and the economic sacrifices made by mothers are viewed as unbearable."

Caldwell's colleague at the Australian National University, Peter McDonald, argues that the southern European phenomenon is a result of the lopsidedness of moves to gender equality. Women have got the freedoms that arise from better education and employment, but not in their relations with their men or in terms of state services for the family. Economic liberalism has clashed with social conservatism. Result: a childbirth strike.

Combining Home and Career

Not all of Europe is quite like Italy, however. In Sweden, for instance, Astrid and her friends feel more able to have a family than Isabella's crowd. They have an average of 1.6 children. That's not enough to maintain their country's population in the long term, but neither is it demographic meltdown. Indeed, most of northern Europe has maintained higher fertility rates than those around the Mediterranean, with Norway at 1.8 and Britain and Finland at 1.7.

Why is Astrid happier to make babies than Isabella? She is just as keen to pursue a career. The difference is that she has more chance of combining a career with motherhood. Her suitors, who are more likely to have set up home on their own before marriage, are better house trained, and Nordic governments are better at helping couples juggle family and work. About half the jobs held by Swedish women are part-time, creches [day nurseries for infants] are near-universal and paid parental leave last for a year. All this is unheard of in Italy, where only 12 percent of employed women have part-time jobs, and in eastern Europe, where fertility rates have plunged since the collapse of communism wrecked state-funded support services for families.

So will the rest of the world follow northern or southern Europe? Caldwell thinks the signs are clear: "The Mediterranean patriarchal model is far more common in the world than the northern European model of more helpful husbands." McDonald says we can already see this in eastern Asia, where conservative family values lie behind the ultra-low fertility rates from Shanghai to Tokyo. Even in Australia, Italian and Greek families are significantly smaller than their Anglo-Saxon counterparts.

One part of the world where fast-falling fertility remains extremely patchy is Africa, where the five- or six-child family is still the norm in many countries. But here another factor is keeping the lid on population growth: AIDS. The UN expects 15 million deaths from AIDS in the next five years, the great majority in Africa. Life expectancy in Botswana and Zimbabwe has plunged from 60 years to close to 40 years.

Birth Rates Fall While Death Rates Rise

In some more economically advanced African countries, birth rates are falling at the same time as death rates are rising. In Kenya, the fertility rate has fallen from 8 to under 5 in two decades, and it could be below 3 within a decade. With AIDS killing off many young children, that could be below the level needed to replace the present population. Kenya could become the first African country with a falling population.

Industrialised countries are already complaining about the effects of falling fertility. An ageing population is putting pressure on social services and pensions. In the next few years they will start to see absolute falls in their populations. Japan expects its population to peak in 2006 and then fall by 14 percent, or almost 20 million people, by 2050. Germany expects a similar drop. Italy and Hungary may lose 25 per cent, and Russia could lose a third by then.

If today's low fertility rates continue, then as the current baby boomers die, things will get drastically worse. If each generation's adults continue to produce not much more than half the number of children needed to replace them, McDonald calculates that the population of Italy is set to crash from 56 million now to just 8 million by 2100. Likewise Spain would lose 85 per cent of its population within the same time frame and Germany 83 per cent.

This year, Charmie and his UN colleagues have been re-drawing population projections on the assumption that the world will move towards an average level of 1.85 children per woman. Much depends on how long this move takes, but according to one of his projections it would result in a world population peaking at about 7.5 billion around 2050. It would then begin to implode. By 2150 there would be 5.3 billion people on the planet. Assume lower future fertility levels and the result is an even more drastic die-off. If women settled for a Swedish-style fertility level of 1.6 children, we would be down to 3.2 billion by 2150—only a fraction over half today's population. Charmie has not yet dared calculate the effect of universal Italian-style fertility.

The Growing Burden of the Elderly

Of course, it may never happen. Some countries seem to have levelled out at above-replacement levels. Argentina and Uruguay, for example, have been stuck at between 2.5 and 3 children per woman for 50 years. Israel and Malaysia stalled at around 3 in the 1990s. Many African countries have not begun the demographic transition yet. And some Muslim states such as Afghanistan (6.9), Saudi Arabia (6.1) and Pakistan (5.5) have also bucked the trend.

Demographers also suspect that if the downward fertility trend continues for much longer, then deep collective instincts of survival could be unmasked. Politicians will grow fearful of the social consequences of declining populations such as the growing burden of supporting the elderly, and an increasing need to find immigrants to augment the labour force.

Such changes will happen in Europe first. "There seems little question that pro-natalist policies will become a central part of the political agenda in the near future," says McDonald. The authoritarian approach would be to try to cut women out of the workforce and keep them at home, to ban abortions, and restrict access to family planning services. But that is unlikely to work, says Dyson. Women wouldn't stand for it. Instead, he argues for a continuation of the "renegotiation" of gender roles underway in much of northern Europe. Paradoxically perhaps, the more feminist attitudes that have helped bring about the dramatic decline in family size in the past 50 years will need extending rather than dismantling if family sizes are to rise from the worst-case Italian model.

But the new agenda may be less about creating new freedoms for women and more about instilling new responsibilities in men and the state. As Dyson puts it, in most of the world today, fertility rates are plunging because women have decided they want to become more like men. Right now that leaves little room for babies. To change that, men must take the plunge and start to become more like women. The future of humanity could depend on it.

Periodical Bibliography

The following articles have been selected to supplement the diverse views presented in this chapter.

Ageless Wisdom	"Abolish Hunger," September 11, 2004. www.theagelesswisdom.com.
Ambassador Agricultural Research Department	"Food vs. Population . . . the Land of Plenty?" October 17, 2001. www.cgca.net.
Nicholas Eberstadt	"Starved for Ideas," American Enterprise Institute, January 1, 2000. www.aei.org.
John Bellamy Foster	"Capitalism and Ecology: The Nature of the Contradiction," *Monthly Review*, September 2002.
Michael Fumento	"The Myth of Too Many," *Citizen*, January 2003.
Roedy Green	"Overpopulation," *Canadian Mind Products*, January 9, 2004. www.mindprod.com.
Russell Hopfenberg and David Pimentel	"Human Population Numbers as a Function of Food Supply," March 6, 2001. www.mnfor sustain.org.
Oneida Kincaid	"Overpopulation and the Problems of Technology," Earth Crash Earth Spirit, November 7, 2001. www.eces.org.
Alex Kirby	"Climate Risk to Million Species," *BBC News*, January 7, 2001. www.bbcnews.com.
Alex Kirby	"Wake-Up Call on Extinction Wave," *BBC News*, August 2003. www.bbcnews.com.
Joseph Klesney	"UN Report Defuses Population Bomb Theory," Acton Institute, June 15, 2000. www.acton.org.
LifeWatch Group	"Practical Solutions to Key World Problems," 2001. www.arrowweb.com.
Anthony LoBaido	"The Overpopulation Lie," May 2, 2000. www.worldnetdaily.com.
Dave Pollard	"Population: A Systems Approach," February 6, 2004. http://blogs.salon.com.
Rehydration Project	"Hunger: Myths and Realities," September 14, 2004. www.rehydrate.org.
James M. Taylor	"UN Study Ends Overpopulation Fears," The Heartland Institute, May 5, 2002. www.heart land.org.

CHAPTER 3

What Are the Effects of Immigration on America's Population?

Chapter Preface

The relationship between immigration and population growth in the United States is hotly debated. One of the central issues in the controversy is what effect immigration-driven population growth has on the environment. When environmentalists discuss population, they most often speak in terms of carrying capacity—the number of people for whom the natural environment of a given area can provide resources, food, clothing, and shelter. The term also refers to the capacity of the social environment to provide a reasonable quality of life. Many researchers and scientists argue that because immigration is currently the greatest source of population growth for the United States, the only way to protect the environment is to severely limit immigration. Scott Czerwonka, coordinator for Population-Environment Balance (BALANCE), a national organization dedicated to maintaining U.S. quality of life through population stabilization, says, "Immigration-driven growth . . . results in over seventy percent of the United States' population increase, and since the United States, too, has a limit on its carrying capacity, excess immigration creates a significant environmental threat."

According to the Federation for American Immigration Reform (FAIR), a national organization that seeks an immigration policy serving America's environmental, economic, and social needs, people from less technologically advanced countries consume resources and degrade the environment more slowly than Americans. However, when immigrants come to the United States, they adopt the American lifestyle and begin to damage the environment at the same rate as native-born citizens. For example, research figures published in 1994 show that immigrants in the United States use up fresh water—a rapidly shrinking resource—at a rate that is 63 percent higher than the rate at which they would be using it in their home countries. Further, immigrants from undeveloped nations triple their energy consumption and their carbon dioxide production when they come to the United States. Thus, proponents of immigration restriction claim, the current high rates of immigration contribute significantly to America's—and the world's—ecological problems.

Environmental degradation due to immigration-driven population increases is just one of the problems central to the debate about U.S. population. Authors in the following chapter debate other significant issues surrounding the relationship between immigration and population growth in the United States.

"*The current large-scale immigration . . .
to the United States . . . is the factor most
responsible for America's unprecedented
population increase.*"

Immigration Is the Main Cause of U.S. Population Increases

Edward Tabash

Edward Tabash argues in the following viewpoint that uncontrolled immigration and the high fertility rates of immigrants are the cause of U.S. overpopulation. Thus, he contends, the United States has a right to restrict immigration in an effort to stabilize its population. Tabash maintains that restricting immigration is not a form of racism but a necessary step that the United States must take to combat the social and ecological problems resulting from overpopulation. Edward Tabash is a constitutional lawyer in Beverly Hills, California. He serves on the board of directors of Californians for Population Stabilization.

As you read, consider the following questions:

1. In Edward Tabash's opinion, why do people equate immigration restriction with racism?
2. If current levels of immigration continue, what figure does the author argue the U.S. population will reach by the end of the century?
3. Who is responsible for the plight of masses of poor Mexicans who want to immigrate to the United States to find a better life, in the author's opinion?

Edward Tabash, "What Population Stabilization Requires," *Free Inquiry*, August/September 2004. Copyright © 2004 by the Council for Democratic and Secular Humanism, Inc. Reproduced by permission.

The godless, naturalistic worldview of secular humanism does not logically compel us to adopt a left-of-center viewpoint on every political issue. Aside from the nonnegotiables—church-state separation and protecting the freedoms that many religious people do not want us to enjoy—nonbelievers may differ on many social and political questions. Notwithstanding the arguments I shall present in this article, I need to stress that ethical and thoughtful people who reject the supernatural can disagree with one another in good faith as to whether or not restricting immigration is a proper approach to reducing U.S. domestic population growth.

A Nation's Right

After a lifetime of fighting the religious Right, I now find myself struggling against a faction on the Left that seems no less impervious to reason. Many on the Left insist that no one can maintain a principled commitment to reducing immigration *as a means of stabilizing runaway U.S. population growth* without being a racist. To make this claim is to commit the same error that religionists do when they assert that no atheist can have a basis for living an ethical life.

I argue that a nation has a right to control the number of people who immigrate to it. If a nation faces massive overpopulation, or if certain regions of that nation face massive overpopulation, national sovereignty allows a government to restrict the number of people who can cross the border. One nation is not required to pay for another's lack of family planning, corruption, or failure to achieve an equitable distribution of wealth by absorbing millions of citizens from that other country.

Mathematically, the current large-scale immigration—both legal and illegal—to the United States and to California in particular, where I reside, is the factor most responsible for America's unprecedented population increase.

California continues to experience massive population growth. One out of every eight people in the United States now lives in the state. Its population is thirty-six million people and grows by about six hundred thousand per year. Immigration, both legal and illegal, is the single most significant factor in California's annual population growth.

Between July 2002 and July 2003, the U.S. Census Bureau estimated that there was a net migration to the United States from other countries of 1,286,118 people, of which 288,051 came to California.

The 2000 census estimated that between eight million and eleven million people then lived in the United States illegally; the number can only have increased since. The Border Patrol reported that between September 30, 2003, and March 31, 2004, its agents detained 535,000 people who had entered the United States illegally from Mexico. (This of course does not include those who managed to enter the United States illegally without being apprehended.) California has a larger number of persons unlawfully present in the country than any other state.

High Immigrant Fertility Rates

Since 1972, the fertility rate of native-born Americans has averaged 10 percent below replacement level. But that of immigrants has averaged *30 percent above* replacement level over the same period. Between 1990 and 2000, the United States endured the greatest census-to-census population increase in the nation's history. Our population grew by 32.7 million people, an increase of 13.2 percent. Almost all of this increase resulted from immigration and the fertility of immigrants. If current levels of immigration continue, the United States could have a population of a billion people by the end of this century.

A sufficient reduction in birthrate would stabilize population growth. But it is legally impermissible to impose mandatory limits on the number of children someone can bear. Thus, the only remaining option for stabilizing population growth is to restrict the number of persons from other countries who enter the United States each year. Accordingly, I believe that the law can and must seek to stabilize population by restricting immigration.

This position is controversial and frequently misunderstood. There is no question that numerous racists and right-wing nuts favor limiting immigration, for all the wrong reasons. But that does nothing to diminish the legitimacy of favoring restricting the annual number of immigrants be-

Liederman. © by Al Liederman. Reproduced by permission of Rothco Cartoons.

cause of valid concerns about overpopulation.

Citizens from other nations do not have a constitutional right to immigrate to the United States, however desperate their circumstances. The heart-wrenching spectacle of teeming masses hazarding fearsome hardships in order to leave Mexico speaks in condemnation of the policies of Mexico's government, not ours. Mexico's wealth remains concentrated among very, very few. Its government has consistently refused to undertake massive efforts to achieve a more equitable distribution of that nation's wealth. Given these facts, and given further Mexico's richness in natural resources, it is Mexico's president, Vicente Fox, and his predecessors who are clearly the true villains in the lives of desperate Mexicans who understandably seek to escape to California or elsewhere in the United States. President Fox is cynical and irresponsible when he chastises the United States for not accepting an ever-increasing number of his own nationals, for whom his government has so miserably failed to provide. To point this out is not racist; it is rational.

Limits of the Safety Net

As a moderate liberal Democrat who believes that government should provide a safety net and social services for the needy, I recognize that there must be a limit to the number of people who can receive these services. If an indigent person lawfully present in California needed expensive medical treatment, it would be understandable to provide that person with that needed care, rather than sending the money to cover the treatment of someone in Norway. This shouldn't change because the person in Norway somehow manages to sneak into the United States. It also shouldn't change if the person who enters the United States illegally happens to come from Mexico.

Rational thought and commonsense problem-solving cannot occur in a climate in which at the moment a logical argument is put forward, opponents characterize it as too evil even to be the subject of debate. This is true whether those opponents are religionists demonizing nonbelievers or leftists mischaracterizing the motives of those who, on environmental grounds, would limit the number of immigrants who come to the United States.

"Most of America's modest population growth today is fueled not by new immigration but by newborn babies."

Immigrants Are Unfairly Blamed for U.S. Population Increases

Daniel T. Griswold

Drastically cutting U.S. immigration in an effort to reduce the population is misguided, Daniel T. Griswold maintains in the following viewpoint. He argues that U.S. population growth is modest, and that what growth exists is due largely to the birth of babies, not immigration. Griswold contends that overcrowding in certain localities and communities is due to the migration of U.S. residents from one area to another, not immigrants coming from other countries to the United States. Daniel T. Griswold is the associate director of the Center for Trade Policy Studies at the Cato Institute, a conservative public policy research foundation.

As you read, consider the following questions:
1. According to the author, what is the trend of U.S. population growth?
2. List two of the reasons that Griswold offers for encouraging immigration.
3. In the author's opinion, what contradictory arguments do opponents of immigration offer?

Television ads airing in a number of cities are trying to blame immigrants for suburban sprawl and traffic jams. One spot playing in northern Virginia, where I live, opens with a pastoral scene of a horse farm and then cuts to a bulldozer tearing up the earth for another subdivision. The ad invites viewers to call "to learn more about what we can do to stop the runaway population growth that's fueling sprawl."

The sponsor of the ad campaign, the Foundation for American Immigration Reform (FAIR), provides a simple but flawed solution: drastically cut immigration to the United States. It would be the wrong answer aimed at the wrong problem.

Newborns Fuel Most U.S. Population Growth

To begin, it mangles the truth to claim that the United States is experiencing "runaway population growth." America's population growth has actually been trending downward for decades. According to the Census Bureau, the population of the United States is growing at just under 1 percent a year. That is slower than the average rate of 1.3 percent during the last century, and far below the peak rate of 1.7 percent in the late 1950s and early 1960s. Our population growth rate is not running away but running down.

Even immigration rates, the real target of the FAIR campaign, are far below their historic highs. During the 1990s, the United States admitted just under four immigrants per year per 1,000 in population. While that rate has been increasing in recent decades, it is still far below the annual rate of 10 immigrants per thousand reached during the Great Migration of 1900–1914. Most of America's modest population growth today is fueled not by new immigrants but by newborn babies.

If you still think your own community is growing too fast, the reason is probably not immigration from abroad, but migration from other cities or states. In fast-growing Loudoun County, Virginia, for example, the *Washington Post* reports that only about 7 percent of newcomers to the county in the 1990s were immigrants. The other 93 percent were U.S. residents who had moved from elsewhere in the region or country.

Immigration Is a Demographic Safety Valve

One of the greatest unheralded economic challenges facing the industrialized nations is the demographic bubble due to unprecedented low birth rates. Economists are just starting to confront the huge economic challenge that the population implosion represents to the developed nations of the world. The birth rates in nations like Japan, Germany, France, Spain, and Italy are well below replacement level fertility. The U.S. is just slightly below replacement level fertility, but we have a demographic safety valve: immigration.

Consider, for example, the level of unfounded liabilities in pension programs around the world. As bad as our Social Security liability problem is, it is dwarfed by the huge levels of red ink in the European nations. Immigration will allow the U.S. to smooth out the bumps in our demographic wave in productive ways that most of our competitor nations will not or cannot allow. Our immigrant heritage allows us to bring in productive immigrant workers, who will help pay the cost of the retirement benefits of everyone . . .

The U.S. legal immigration system works remarkably well, given that it has been crafted in a piecemeal way over many years. Most immigrants who come to the U.S. today are economic contributors on net. The system of family and employer sponsored immigration is effective in getting high quality immigrants to come to the U.S. and absorbing them rapidly into the labor force and the culture. Immigrant workers have brought a flexibility and a work ethic to the U.S. labor market that is sorely absent in many of our major competitor nations.

It is noteworthy that it was not so many years ago that anti-immigration groups would point glowingly to Japan as an example of a nation that prospers without immigration. Japan is now entering its second decade of depression. Part of the problem in Japan has been economic policy mistakes. But some of its economic maladies are a result of low birth rates. Also, the aging of the workforce in Japan is a horrendous demographic crisis in that nation. The absence of immigrants in Japan has already come to haunt this once formidable economic powerhouse.

Stephen Moore, testimony before the Senate Judiciary Committee Subcommitee on Immigration, April 4, 2001.

Immigrants add to the economic vitality of communities where they locate. Why is that a problem? They promote local business expansion by raising demand for products and by providing labor, technical skills, entrepreneurial talent, and international business connections. For existing home-owners, economic growth and expanding populations increase demand for housing raising property values. Behind the pejorative label, "sprawl" is just another way of describing the growth of jobs and incomes and the resulting rise in demand for new single-family homes.

For all these reasons, attracting immigrants has become an important part of state and local development plans, especially in more rural regions where population growth has slowed or even reversed. In Iowa, for example, it has become an official part of the state's economic development strategy to promote immigration. For most communities in the United States, economic growth is not a problem to be solved, but a blessing to be sought.

Immigration Is a Blessing

As for traffic congestion, the real problem is not too many immigrants but a government-managed transportation system that is slow to respond to changing needs. Bureaucracy, politics and costly labor regulations and domestic purchase requirements all conspire to delay completion and drive up the cost of highway improvements. A more market-driven transportation system, not controls on growth or immigration, should be the preferred response to traffic congestion. After all, Rome and Tokyo suffer from terrible traffic even though immigration rates in Italy and Japan are among the lowest in the world.

Opponents of immigration are tangling themselves in contradictory arguments. They contend, despite ample evidence to the contrary, that immigration somehow lowers wages, pushes Americans out of jobs, and reduces property values, hurting local economies where immigrants settle. Yet they also argue that immigrants fuel growth and development, and all the problems that supposedly come with them.

The truth is that immigration has been a great blessing, to America as a whole and to the local communities where immigrants make their homes. If the people behind the FAIR ads have their way, America will face problems far greater than too many new jobs and new homes.

"An increasingly large percentage of those pouring through our borders are undereducated, unskilled workers who threaten the income of blue-collar workers."

Immigration Increases Unemployment

Steve Gill

A ballooning population caused by uncontrolled immigration is driving high rates of U.S. unemployment, Steve Gill claims in the following viewpoint. He maintains that not only do immigrants take jobs from American citizens, unskilled immigrants also drive wages down because they are willing to work for less money. Gill insists that the government must take immediate action to stop illegal immigration and restrict legal immigration if American jobs are to be saved. Steve Gill is a radio and television talk show host in Nashville, Tennessee.

As you read, consider the following questions:
1. According to Gill, how many legal immigrants does the government allow into the United States each year?
2. In the author's opinion, why do most immigrants come to the United States?
3. Who pays for the cost of immigration, according to the author?

Steve Gill, "Immigrants Passing Out Pink Slips," *The Tullahoma News*, October 14, 2003. Copyright © 2003 by *The Tullahoma News*. Reproduced by permission.

Millions of hard-working Americans who are desperate for jobs can't find them, and both the short term and long term prospects do not bode well for many American workers.

The economic problems we face would be bad enough if all we had to contend with were a recovering economy, the continued threat of terrorism, and increased competition from foreign companies.

Immigrants Take Jobs from Unskilled Workers

But a Congress that should be looking for ways to help unemployed Americans is busy opening the floodgates to millions of new immigrants who take jobs away from Americans—and also helping companies take the remaining jobs offshore.

It almost appears that our government is committed to making sure everybody in the world has a job—except Americans.

Historically, the U.S. admitted around 300,000 legal immigrants per year, but Congress changed our immigration policies back around 1965 and opened the floodgates. We now allow more than a *million* legal immigrants into the country each year. A small number of these are refugees; some have special skills not easily found here. But an increasingly large percentage of those pouring through our borders are undereducated, unskilled workers who threaten the income of blue-collar workers, the backbone of America. Millions more come here each year *illegally*, and the government does nothing to stop that either.

It's no secret that most immigrants—legal and illegal— come to the United States for a single reason: money. They know that no matter what a job pays here, it will be far more than they could ever hope to earn in their own country. A job in America is a ticket to what appears to them to be fortune, letting them live better than they could have imagined at home.

It's also no secret that those same immigrants will underbid any American for any job. Their arrival by the thousands corresponds directly with thousands of Americans being pushed out of a job. In effect, every visa given to an unskilled foreigner is really a pink slip handed to a hard-working American. Worse yet, the pink slips are being handed to Americans by their own government, paid for with their own tax money!

Immigrants Take American Jobs

Northeastern University's recent study of immigrants in the U.S. labor force, which . . . shows that immigrants are crowding Americans out of the job market, also presents fresh evidence for this immigrant impact on American wages.

Looking at just those immigrant workers that came to the U.S. since 2000, the Northeastern labor economists found:

• 35 percent hadn't graduated high school, versus 11 percent of all U.S.-born workers

• 28 percent had a BA or higher degree, slightly above the ratio for U.S.-born workers

Edwin S. Rubenstein, *National Data*, www.vdare.com, August 17, 2004.

And the cost of this flood of immigration is not just being borne by those who lose their jobs. American taxpayers are increasingly funding the health, education and welfare of millions of immigrants at a cost of tens of billions of dollars per year. The Federation for American Immigration Reform recently released a report that detailed the fact that educating illegal alien children is costing the U.S. over $7 billion a year—enough to buy a computer for every middle school child in America. Health care for the two million illegals in California runs in the billions of dollars a year; and it is estimated that the annual health care costs of delivering illegal alien children in Denver, Colorado alone is in excess of ten million dollars. All of these costs are borne by American taxpayers.

Congress Must Take Action

Clearly, we have a broken system, one that lets hundreds of thousands of unskilled immigrants—legal and illegal—into the United States at random to take Americans jobs, stifle the American economy, and put little or nothing back into strained local, state and federal tax coffers.

This has to end. Congress needs to immediately enforce our immigration laws to stop the flood of illegal immigration and change our outdated laws to reduce legal immigration back to more manageable numbers. A step in the right direction is a bill introduced by Rep. Bob Goodlatte of Virginia, H.R. 775,[1] which would end the totally unnecessary visa lottery program. It would help give us a "time out" while we assess other ways to manage immigration into this country.

America has always been a land of opportunity and a nation of immigrants. But when the opportunity is for today's flood of immigrants to put Americans on the unemployment line, our system is out of whack. Instead of maintaining policies that hand out pink slips to America, Congress needs to get serious about stopping illegal immigration and reduce legal immigration to reasonable levels that will allow the millions who have flooded into this country in recent years to assimilate. Every day of delay is another stack of pink slips for Americans.

---

1. H.R. 775, the Security and Fairness Enhancement Act of 2003, is an amendment to the Immigrant and Naturalization Act, which eliminates the diversity immigrant program. On September 14, 2004, the bill was forwarded from the Subcommitee on Immigration, Border Security and Claims to the Full Committee of the House Judiciary.

"Neither U.S. workers nor most minority workers appear adversely affected by immigration."

Immigration Does Not Increase Unemployment

Michael Tanner

Michael Tanner argues in the following viewpoint that immigrants do not take jobs from American citizens nor do they drive down wages. In fact, Tanner contends, the influx of immigrants to a particular area helps create jobs. Further, he maintains that immigrants tend to be more entrepreneurial than native-born Americans and often start new businesses. Tanner insists that immigrants also use welfare at a lower rate than do native-born Americans, thus causing less of a drain on taxpayers. Michael Tanner is the director of Health and Welfare Studies at the Cato Institute, a conservative public policy research foundation.

As you read, consider the following questions:

1. What three characteristics of immigrants does the author argue will help advance the economic well-being of all Americans?
2. List two ways that, according to the author, immigrants help create jobs.
3. What does Tanner maintain is the best way to limit the impact of immigrants on states and localities where they settle?

America has always been a nation of immigrants. Thomas Jefferson emphasized this basic part of the American heritage, taking note of "the natural right which all men have of relinquishing the country in which birth or other accident may have thrown them, and seeking subsistence and happiness wheresoever they may be able, and hope to find them."

Immigrants Help Create Jobs

The Libertarian Party has long recognized the importance of allowing free and open immigration, understanding that this leads to a growing and more prosperous America. We condemn the xenophobic immigrant bashing that would build a wall around the United States. At the same time, we recognize that the right to enter the United States does not include the right to economic entitlements such as welfare. The freedom to immigrate is a freedom of opportunity, not a guarantee of a handout.

A policy of open immigration will advance the economic well-being of all Americans. All major recent studies of immigrants indicate that they have a high labor force participation, are entrepreneurial, and tend to have specialized skills that allow them to enter under-served markets. Although it is a common misconception that immigrants "take jobs away from native-born Americans," this does not appear to be true. In 1989, the U.S. Department of Labor reviewed nearly 100 studies on the relationship between immigration and unemployment and concluded that "neither U.S. workers nor most minority workers appear adversely affected by immigration."

Indeed, most studies show that immigrants actually lead to an increase in the number of jobs available. Immigrants produce jobs in several ways: 1) They expand the demand for goods and services through their own consumption; 2) They bring savings with them that contribute to overall investment and productivity; 3) They are more highly entrepreneurial than native-born Americans and create jobs through the businesses they start; 4) They fill gaps in the low and high ends of the labor markets, producing subsidiary jobs for American workers; 5) Low-wage immigrants may enable threatened American businesses to survive competition from low-wage businesses abroad; and 6) They contribute to increased economic efficiencies through economies of scale.

Confirmation can be seen in a study by economists Richard Vedder and Lowell Galloway of Ohio University and Stephen Moore of the Cato Institute [a conservative public policy research foundation]. They found that states with the highest rates of immigration during the 1980s also had the highest rates of economic growth and lowest rates of unemployment.

Immigration Has Little Effect on Wages

Studies also show that not only do immigrants not take jobs away from American workers, they also do not drive down wages. Numerous studies have demonstrated that increased immigration has little or no effect on the wages of most American workers, and may even increase wages at upper income levels.

Contrary to stereotypes, there is no evidence that immigrants come to this country to receive welfare. Indeed, most studies show that immigrants actually use welfare at lower rates than do native-born Americans. For example, a study of welfare recipients in New York City found that only 7.7% of immigrants were receiving welfare compared to 13.3% for the population as a whole. Likewise, a nationwide study by the U.S. Bureau of Labor Statistics found that 12.8% of immigrants were receiving welfare benefits, compared to 13.9% of the general population. Some recent studies indicate that the rate of welfare usage may now be equalizing between immigrants and native-born Americans, but, clearly, most immigrants are not on welfare.

The impact of immigrants on taxes is more equivocal. Most immigrants pay more in taxes than they receive in government benefits. However, the majority of immigrant taxes are paid to the federal government, while immigrants tend to use mostly state and local services. This can place a burden on states and localities in high immigration areas.

However, the answer to this problem lies not in cutting off immigration, but in cutting the services that immigrants consume. The right to immigrate does not imply a right to welfare—or any other government service. Moreover, this is not

Immigration Is a Safety Valve

Immigrants play an important part in the success of America's free-enterprise economy, filling important niches in the labor market. Immigrants gravitate to occupations where the gap between the supply of workers and demand for them is greatest, typically in the highest-skilled and lowest-skilled jobs. That hourglass shape of the immigration labor pool complements the native workforce, where most workers fall in the middle range in terms of skills and education. As a result, immigrants do not compete directly with the vast majority of American workers.

Immigration provides a safety valve for the U.S. labor market, allowing the supply of workers to increase relatively quickly to meet rising demand. When demand fails, would-be immigrants can decide not to enter, and those already here can decide to return home. The result is a more efficient economy that can achieve a higher rate of sustainable growth without encountering bottlenecks or stoking inflation.

The impact of immigration on the relatively small segment of the workforce that competes directly with immigrants is more than offset by the lower prices that all workers enjoy for the goods produced by immigrants, and by the higher return on investment. The comprehensive study by National Research Council in 1997 concluded that immigration delivers a "significant positive gain" of $1 billion to $10 billion a year to native Americans. And those gains from immigration recur year after year.

Daniel T. Griswold, testimony before the House Subcommittee on Immigration, Border Security and Claims, www.freetrade.org, October 30, 2003.

simply a matter of saving tax money. The Libertarian Party believes that most government welfare programs are destructive to the recipients themselves. Thus, immigrants would actually be better off without access to these programs. As Edward Crane, President of the Cato Institute, has put it:

"Suppose we increased the level of immigration, but the rule would be that immigrants and their descendants would have no access to government social services, including welfare, Social Security, health care, business subsidies, and the public schools. I would argue, first, that there would be no lack of takers for that proposition. Second, within a generation, we would see those immigrants' children going to better and cheaper schools than the average citizen; there would be less poverty, a better work ethic, and proportionately more entrepreneurs than in the rest of U.S. society; and virtually everyone in that group would have inexpensive high-deductible catastropic health insurance, while the 'truly needy' would be cared for by an immigrarant culture that gave proportinately more to charity."

An Obsession with Immigration Restriction

Finally, any discussion of immigration must include a warning about the threat to civil liberties posed by many of the proposals to limit immigration. Recent legislation to restrict immigration has included calls for a national identity card for all Americans. Senator Dianne Feinstein (D-CA) has suggested that such an ID card should contain an individual's photograph, fingerprints, and even retina scans. Representative Lamar Smith (R-TX) has proposed legislation that would require employers to consult a national registry of workers before hiring anyone, effectively giving the U.S. government control over every hiring decision by every business in America.

Other legislation has contained provisions penalizing people who fail to "inform" on people they "suspect" might be illegal immigrants. Such Orwellian nightmares have no place in a free society, but are the natural outgrowth of an obsession with restricting immigration.

"Our broken immigration system combined with multiculturalism is eroding America's sovereignty and the national identity of its citizens."

Population Increases Resulting from Immigration Undermine National Unity

Rob Sobhani

The flawed American immigration system is allowing too many immigrants into the country, which is adding to existing population problems, crowding out native-born citizens who need the same services, and undermining American culture, Rob Sobhani argues in the following viewpoint. He maintains that most recent immigrants are coming to the United States to escape poverty and corrupt governments in their homelands with no intention of becoming loyal Americans. Further, Sobhani insists that liberals' emphasis on multiculturalism encourages immigrants to retain their own culture rather than accepting American ways. Rob Sobhani is an adjunct professor at Georgetown University.

As you read, consider the following questions:

1. In Rob Sobhani's opinion, why do recent immigrants have little incentive to become Americans?
2. What does the author argue should be the new name of the Immigration and Naturalization Service?
3. How does large-scale immigration impact America's black and native American communities, in Sobhani's opinion?

The House [of Representatives] vote to abolish the INS [Immigration and Naturalization Service] and split it into two bureaus completely fails to address the root problems America faces as a result of its broken immigration policy. The 1990s mass immigration to America is the result of foreign policy directives that failed to address the core problems of freedom, economic opportunity, and corruption in countries like Mexico, Egypt, Iran, Pakistan, Russia, India, and the Philippines, among others. With few exceptions, the citizens of these countries come to America to escape poverty, repression and corruption, *not necessarily to become Americans.*

Furthermore, our broken immigration system combined with multiculturalism is eroding America's sovereignty and the national identity of its citizens. Once in America, recent immigrants have little incentive to become Americans because the liberal culture tells them that we are a multicultural nation of immigrants rather than a nation of people from many different countries embracing the American culture. Separation, not assimilation, has become the norm: Mexican-American; Pakistani-American; Arab-American; Chinese-American. This hyphenation of America can only lead to the creation of divided loyalties, which only plays into the hands of America's enemies, of which there are many.

The INS Must Be Reformed

If our elected officials are serious about 1) protecting America's borders, 2) increasing security at home, 3) creating jobs instead of handouts for America's disadvantaged, and 4) preserving our national unity, then any reform needs to address the following issues.

First, since symbolism is important, renaming the bureau responsible for assimilating newly arrived immigrants to "The Immigration and Americanization Service" is a good start.

Second, language is the glue that holds a country together. English must become the official language of America. It is the language of our Constitution and the language of economic opportunity. Unfortunately, both political parties have started a shameful policy of pandering to recent immigrants (especially Mexicans) by allowing for a dual-language system. In my home state of Maryland, you can take a driver's license

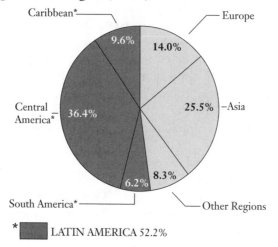

Foreign-Born People in the United States by Region of Origin (2002)

Caribbean* 9.6%

Europe 14.0%

Asia 25.5%

Central America* 36.4%

South America* 6.2%

Other Regions 8.3%

* LATIN AMERICA 52.2%

U.S. Bureau of the Census, www.census.gov, 2002.

exam in Spanish, but why not in Hebrew or Turkish?

Third, loyalty to America matters, especially after the national calamity of September 11 [2001, when Arab terrorists attacked the United States]. We should not apologize for asking immigrants to be patriotic. The Pledge of Allegiance should once more be a mandatory part of every child's school day. Swearing-in ceremonies for new American citizens must be administered only in English and not in any other language. The citizenship exams—which today only require the prospective citizen to identify their senators and congressmen—must include questions about the history of America and its Constitution. The issue of dual citizenship must also be seriously questioned.

The Family Reunification Issue

Fourth, since the basis of our current immigration policy is "family reunification," when one member of an immigrant family gains a foothold he or she begins a chain migration by bringing in the entire extended family. This places an enormous burden on our nation's resources. Family members of recent immigrants expect access to Medicare and Medicaid.

The demands on the public-school system are staggering due to explosive growth in the population of new immigrant children. Counties throughout America are struggling to pay for the education of millions of these new immigrant children, not to mention a bilingual-education bureaucracy that has been forced upon them. This crowding out of precious resources for elderly and disadvantaged Americans is a consequence of a failed immigration policy that can only be addressed by a temporary moratorium on immigrant visas to the United States.

The American economy would receive an enormous boost if we cut back on immigrant visas and instead focused on the issuance of visitors' visas (another form of family unification without the cost to American taxpayers) and student visas. Both visas would be temporary. Visitors would spend money and students would learn about America. Both would eventually have to return. Of course, it is crucial that the new immigration office devise strict guidelines governing who is allowed into America and then ensuring that they do not overstay their visas.

Fifth, one of America's top moral priorities is the healing of America's black and native-American communities. To the extent that the large-scale immigration of the 1990s (illegal as well as legal) interferes with meeting black American's socioeconomic needs, immigration reform must address the correlation between black employment and immigration. Consider what Mark Krikorian of the Center for Immigration Studies calls "the intersection of affirmative action and immigration." Since minority status is fungible and any kind of minority status counts towards the goal of affirmative action, businesses have avoided hiring blacks simply by hiring immigrants. Therefore, under the banner of diversity, a window of opportunity has opened for recent immigrants (primarily Hispanics and Asians) and that same window has been slammed shut on the black underclass. In short, affirmative action's black-centered rationale is being undermined by mass immigration.

America's out-of-control immigration policy should be addressed immediately by both the Congress and the White House before our country becomes the Balkanized States of America instead of the United States of America.

> "Hispanic immigrants uproot themselves
> . . . not in order to re-create their own
> country in the United States, but to learn
> America's ways of success."

Population Increases Resulting from Immigration Do Not Undermine National Unity

Henry Cisneros

The large and continuing influx of legal and illegal immigrants poses no threat to American culture and instead will likely strengthen it, Henry Cisneros argues in the following viewpoint. He contends that despite their immense numbers, immigrants who come to the United States are ready to accept American values such as democracy, respect for personal liberty and private property, free enterprise, and personal accomplishment. They will therefore enhance national unity, not detract from it, he maintains. Henry Cisneros is the former secretary of the Department of Housing and Urban Development.

As you read, consider the following questions:
1. In the author's opinion, why are those who argue that the United States will become divided into a country of two cultures and two languages wrong?
2. What is one of the most powerful dimensions of Hispanic immigration, according to Henry Cisneros?
3. Name three contributions that Hispanic immigration has brought to metropolitan areas such as New York, Chicago, and Los Angeles, according to Cisneros.

The central thesis of Harvard Professor Samuel Huntington's book, *Who Are We?*, is his claim that "the single most immediate and most serious challenge to America's traditional identity comes from the immense and continuing immigration from Latin America, especially from Mexico, and the fertility rates of these immigrants compared to black and white American natives."

He raises fears that the United States will not remain "a country with a single language and a core Anglo-Protestant culture," but become transformed into two cultures and two languages.

Old Fears About Immigration

Huntington's polemic is the latest expression in a long history of alarms about immigration to the United States. As successive waves of immigrants arrived in the United States over two centuries—Irish, Italians, Jews, Chinese, Germans, Eastern Europeans and many others—they were always greeted by nativist protests targeted against the different languages, appearances, religions and lifestyles, and against the workplace competitiveness of the new arrivals. Europeans today are familiar with the anger and fear directed at immigrants in various continental countries.

But Huntington says that his analysis is different from the time-worn and predictable screeds, because this wave of immigration is so profoundly different from any before it and therefore more dangerous to American identity. He postulates six reasons why he believes the successes of past immigration are irrelevant to the present situation. They are:

• Contiguity: the fact that the United States shares a porous 2,000-mile border with Mexico.

• Scale: that Hispanics total about one-half of all immigrants entering the United States, so that for the first time in U.S. history, half of those entering the nation "speak a single non-English language."

• Illegality: that estimates of Mexican illegal immigrants, which ranged as high as 350,000 per year in the 1990s, mean that today an estimated 4.8 million Mexicans make up 69 percent of the illegal population.

• Regional concentration: that the proportions of Hispanics continue to grow in the regions of heaviest residence, such as the Southwestern states and California.

• Persistence: that the current wave of Hispanic immigration shows no signs of slowing.

• Historical presence: that because major parts of the American Southwest were once part of Mexico, "Mexican Americans enjoy a sense of being on their own turf that is not shared by other immigrants."

Certain of Huntington's six points are matters of unarguable fact, such as that the United States shares a 2,000-mile border with Mexico. Other points are matters of conjecture, such as whether immigration flows will be persistent or will be sustained at the scale of recent years, because the flows depend on relative economic conditions in the sending nations and on the scale of the demand for workers in the United States in years to come. But it is in drawing his overarching conclusions from these six points that Huntington goes badly off course.

The Strength of American Culture

Unfortunately, as with navigating across a great sea, a few degrees of misjudgment here, a few degrees of miscalculation there, and a few degrees of plain old wrong-headedness in the end will bring the ship out in a very strange place.

If Columbus had used Huntington's method of reckoning, there would be no United States to worry about its immigrant history because this land would still be in the hands of the Native Americans, and Columbus would have searched for gold in Antarctica.

Huntington comes out so wrong for an ironic reason: He doesn't ascribe enough strength to America's culture, the attraction of its way of life or the power of its institutions.

Each immigrant has made a personal calculation that life in the United States is better than life in his or her own country and has acted upon that conviction. Today's Hispanic immigrants uproot themselves, disrupt the lives of loved ones, confront dangers and face new circumstances not in order to re-create their own country in the United States, but to learn America's ways of success and progress.

That personal commitment to work and striving repeated

millions of times is a powerful source of energy for the American future. In amazingly few years, Hispanic immigrants and their children adapt language, work practices and lifestyles to the American way. They serve patriotically in America's armed forces, they pay taxes, they revitalize neighborhoods, they sustain entire industries and they make consumer products affordable by their hard work.

American Traditions Are Based on Ideas

There is another flaw lurking in the argument that open immigration leads to the decline of a nation's cultural and institutional framework. Contrary to the anti-immigration position, the American traditions of limited government and free market economies are not based upon ethnic or racial origins. They are based upon ideas. Western cultures cannot suppose themselves to have a monopoly on the philosophy of liberty, nor can Americans argue that the political values of the limited state cannot be inculcated in non-American immigrants. The ideas of freedom that have created the American tradition can apply to any ethnic or racial make-up.

Thomas E. Lehman, *The Freeman*, December 1995.

In characterizing the new Hispanic immigrants strictly in terms of their first language or their lack of Anglo-Protestant lineage, Huntington neglects one of the most powerful dimensions of Hispanic immigration: Hispanics in America are young, statistically more youthful than the national average age.

Therefore, while Japan, Germany, France and Italy project dramatically slower rates of growth for their populations and labor forces—with unknown implications for their economies—the United States is gaining a youthful workforce, new family formations, emerging markets and energetic, ambitious young leaders.

In his hand-wringing over the tainting of Anglo-Protestant bloodlines, Huntington overlooks the impressive evidence from America's most successful cities that diversity of population is a driving force in the new economy. Diversity has become a building block of the new paradigm of economic development, as the interweaving of backgrounds and perspectives contribute to creativity and the convergence of fresh ideas and productive streams of thought generate economic momentum. Metropolitan areas from New York to Chicago to Los Angeles, and many smaller cities in between, are experiencing solid population growth, surging retail trade and exploding entrepreneurship due to Hispanic immigration. That immigrant-fueled diversity is also making it possible for the United States to build bridges of commercial and cultural exchange to other parts of the world.

America's Fundamental Identity

The greatest error in Huntington's alarmist conclusions, however, is that he misunderstands America's fundamental identity. It is not an identity based on how people look, or what language they learned first, or over how many generations their absorption of Anglo-Protestant values occurred. Rather, America's is an identity based upon acceptance of the rules of law and of democratic processes of lawmaking; of respect for personal liberty and private property; of understanding our system of free enterprise and adopting our national narrative of striving and accomplishment. It has been my experience that those values the newest immigrants accept enthusiastically. After all, those values are why they took the trouble to come.

Periodical Bibliography

The following articles have been selected to supplement the diverse views presented in this chapter.

B. Meredith Burke	"Immigration's Dire Effect on the Environment," *Seattle Times*, June 15, 2000.
Mark Nathan Cohen	"Carrying Capacity," *Free Inquiry*, August/September 2004.
Chris Crass	"Controlling Gendered Immigrants and Racialized Populations: Overpopulation, Immigration, and Environmental Sustainability," April 27, 2000. www.infoshop.org.
Julie Delcour	"It's in the Numbers: Is the Melting Pot Facing a Meltdown?" *Tulsa World*, December 2, 2001.
Federation for American Immigration Reform	"How Do Environmental Groups Rank Regarding Immigration?" April 2003. www.fairus.org.
Laura L. Garcia	"The Globalization of Family Planning," *World & I*, December 2000.
Daniel T. Griswold	"No: Immigrants Have Enriched American Culture and Enhanced Our Influence in the World," *Insight*, February 18, 2002.
Joe Guzzardi	"The Consequences of Mass Immigration," December 8, 2002. www.calnews.com.
Betsy Hartmann	"Conserving Racism: The Greening of Hate at Home and Abroad," December 10, 2003. www.zmag.org.
Alan Kuper	"The Silent Crisis," *Free Inquiry*, August/September 2004.
Richard D. Lamm	"Why I'm Running: Immigration Is the Environmental Issue," *High Country News*, February 16, 2004.
Yeh Ling-Ling	"Averting an Immigration Time Bomb," 2004. www.wisdomsociety.org.
Dale Lovell	"The Problem of Europe's Ageing Population," *Contemporary Review*, May 2004.
New York Times	"Blaming Immigrants," October 14, 2000.
David Simcox	"Amnesty: Overpopulation by Fiat," *Negative Population Growth Forum Series*, November 2002.

Jack C. Terrazas and
Yeh Ling-Ling

"A Common Sense Immigration Policy," 2004.
www.wisdomsociety.org.

Michael J. Thompson

"Immigration Cause of America's Problems,"
Auburn Plainsman, March 20, 2003.

John Wall

"Blame an Immigrant," October 2000. www.
vdare.com.

CHAPTER 4

What Population Policies Should Be Pursued?

Chapter Preface

The Programme of Action developed by the International Conference on Population and Development (ICPD) held in Cairo in 1994 represented a significant change in the way the world viewed the relationship between population stabilization, economic development, and health. The Programme of Action put particular emphasis on the health, well-being, and empowerment of women as a crucial aspect of least developed countries' push for sustainable development and an end to poverty. The Programme of Action refused to condone the coercive population control policies, such as forced serialization and one-child-only policies, that had been supported in prior decades. Many attending the conference predicted that this sea change in thinking about population problems would have far-reaching consequences. Nafis Sadik, United Nations Population Fund (UNFPA) executive director and secretary-general of the conference, said at the closing session, "The Programme contains highly specific goals and recommendations in the mutually reinforcing areas of infant and maternal mortality, education, and reproductive health and family planning, but its effect will be far wider ranging than that. This Programme of Action has the potential to change the world."

The UNFPA conducted a global survey of governments in 2003 to determine just how much the world had been changed by the Programme of Action. The UNFPA survey found that 99 percent of the least developed countries responding to the survey indicated that they had created new policies, laws, or constitutional amendments protecting the rights of women and girls, promoting female education, and opposing all gender-based violence. Further, most of the countries have begun to include reproductive health services—including family planning for both men and women—in primary health-care initiatives.

Only time will determine whether these statistics translate into better lives for the citizens of poor countries. The effectiveness of the Programme of Action is just one of the issues authors in the following chapter explore as they debate the most effective global population policies for the twenty-first century.

"To harness the benefits of economic development and maximise its impact on . . . individuals, it is essential that the population base of the State be limited."

Governments Should Promote Population Control

K. Prasada Rao

In the following viewpoint K. Prasada Rao argues that government-backed population control is necessary for India's economic development. He maintains that government support—including public health centers that provide sterilization operations, dispense birth control, and counsel girls to wait until their late teens to marry—have helped India make great economic and social strides. K. Prasada Rao is the minister of health at the Department of Medical, Health, and Family Welfare of the Indian state of Andhra Pradesh.

As you read, consider the following questions:

1. According to the author, when did Andhra Pradesh adopt its State Population Policy?
2. What did the Andhra Pradesh government do to reinforce the acceptance of sterilization as a method of maintaining small family size and help ensure child survival, according to Rao?
3. What incentive does the author report the government offers poor women to encourage them to choose to have their babies in hospitals (institutional deliveries) rather than at home?

K. Prasada Rao, speech given at the Conference of State Population Commissions/Councils, September 25, 2002. Copyright © 2002 by the National Commission on Population. Reproduced by permission.

In order to harness the benefits of economic development and maximise its impact on the lives of individuals, it is essential that the population base of the State be limited. Population stabilisation therefore assumes great significance in this context. AP [Andhra Pradesh State in India] adopted the State Population Policy in early 1997 and it marked the beginning of an intensive effort to stabilize the population. Ambitious goals were set and [a] reproductive and child health approach was adopted to achieve population stabilisation. This approach, besides being pro-women and children, also highlights the necessity of making quality focused, client driven services widely available to achieve the population goals.

The initiatives of the Government have already yielded results and it is reflected in the Census of 2001, which highlights some of the important achievements of AP. AP recorded an amazing fall in the decadal population growth rate. While the all-India decadal population growth rate fell from 23.86% in 1991 to 21.34% in 2001, AP registered the steepest fall in the country from 24.2% in 1991 to 13.86% in 2001. Further there has been a remarkable decline in the Total Fertility Rate from 4 per woman in 1981 to 2.25 in 1998.

All Levels of Governments Are Involved

To translate the challenging goals into activities we put the entire State machinery into action. The involvement of all political representatives from the CM [Chief Minister] to the Sarpanch [head of the village council] irrespective of party affiliations ensured that a people's movement is generated. Step-by-step, gaining in strength with each day, awareness of the small family norm permeated into every household in Andhra Pradesh. Simultaneously, improving the women's status economically and politically was given a very high priority. As a result, women became conscious of concerns related to health, education and nutrition of their families and took decisions about their family size.

Another factor for the success was the effort made by the district administration and the health staff to make the family planning services widely available all over the State, even in the remote areas. The Government which had banned all recruitment, continued to fill-up vacancies of doctors and paramedical staff. New buildings were constructed for Public Health Centers [PHC] and supply of drugs and consumables enhanced and streamlined. Most of the PHCs became centres for all family planning services, including sterilization operations. A large number of doctors were trained in the new techniques for family planning operations. A key role has also been played by the ANM [female nurses trained in Auxiliary Nursing and Midwifery classes] at the field level. She has been in the forefront in providing services for children, pregnant women and in counselling eligible couples.

All these efforts have combined to gain wide acceptance of the small family norm across the State, taking our family planning operations from 5.14 lakhs [514,000] in 1996–97 to more than eight lakhs [800,000] per year since 2000–01. To reinforce the acceptance of small family norm and ensure child survival, we introduced the Aarogyaraksha Scheme, which provides insurance for a period of 5 years from the time of operation for the family planning acceptor and his or her 2 children.

Improving Reproductive Health

Besides providing family planning services, we have also concentrated on improving the reproductive and child health of couples and children in the State. The focus is now on age at marriage, spacing, institutional delivery and immunisation. There is now a campaign running on age at marriage. Trainings are being conducted for women, adolescent girls and opinion leaders on the issue of age at marriage.

A high priority is now accorded to improve institutional deliveries. The facilities provided by the referral hospitals were improved and PHCs in rural, interior and backward areas were designated as Round the Clock Women Health Centres. Maternal [and] child care services are being provided round the clock in these institutions. The ANMs are on turn duty in 3 shifts to attend deliveries 24 hours. Specialist services of gynecologist and pediatrician are being provided in these institutions once weekly. Additional facilities like phone . . . are also allotted to improve communication and referral system for emergency cases. I am glad to mention that the number of institutional deliveries has in-

Provisional Population Totals: Andhra Pradesh

The total population of Andhra Pradesh as at 0:00 hours of 1st March 2001 stood at 75,727,541 as per the provisional results of the Census of India 2001. Andhra Pradesh has relegated to fifth most populous State in the country as against fourth returned at the previous census. This [state] has achieved substantial reduction in its decadal growth of population during the decade 1991–2001. While country's decadal growth rate of population is 21.34%, Andhra Pradesh has registered an increase of only 13.86% between 1991–2001. The State has also shown downward trend in its growth of population over the previous decade. Decade 1981–1991 witnessed an increase of 24.20% in population, which allowed down to 13.86% during 1991–2001.

Population:

Persons	75,727,541
Males	38,286,811
Females	37,440,730
Sex Ratio:	978

Decadal Growth 1991–2001:

Persons:	(+) 13.86%
Males:	(+) 13.53%
Females:	(+) 14.21%

Population (0–6 years):

Persons	9,673,274
Males	4,926,200
Females	4,747,074
Sex Ratio:	964
(0–6 years)	

Percentage of Population (0–6) to Total Population:

Persons:	12.77%
Males:	12.87%
Females:	12.68%

Numer of Literates:

Persons	40,364,765
Males	23,636,077
Females	16,728,688

Percentage of Literates to Total Population:

Persons:	61.11%
Males:	70.85%
Females:	51.17%

Provisional Population Totals: India. Census of India 2001, Paper 1 of 2001. www.censusindia.net.

creased drastically in the PHCs from 64227 in 2000–01 to 121153 in 2001–02. The reported institutional deliveries have shown a jump from 49% in 98–99 to 65% in 2001–02. [The] Sukhibhava scheme to support poor women to opt for institutional deliveries has been introduced consciously. Under this scheme, women below poverty line residing in rural area are paid Rs. [Indian Rupee] 300 [about six dollars and fifty cents] towards transport charges and incidental expenses if they have delivery in any government institution. Rs. 10 Crores [slightly more than two million dollars] is the budget for 2001–2002.

To strengthen the children's immunisation, we have had a serious look at the Programme implementation. Besides introducing the Hepatitis B vaccine and expanding safe injection practices, gaps in drugs, consumables [and] logistics related to immunization are being identified [and] filled. We are consolidating the institution of ANM, by upgrading her skills and providing her additional drugs. We intend to position additional ANMs. To ensure improved outreach services by the ANMs we are giving our support from the Sarpanch and self-help groups in the form of mother [and] child health care team at the village level. Further, few ANMs are provided with mopeds and provision of palm tops of the ANMs for mechanized data storage and retrieval is being piloted.

Establishment of Urban Health Centers

As the usage of spacing methods in AP is one of the lowest in the country and probably contributing to the maternal and child deaths, we are implementing a contraceptive social marketing programme. Under this programme, over 1.5 lakh [150 thousand] SHG [Self-Help Groups] members have been trained on spacing methods, 16000 depots have been established and around 50 franchisee clinics that provide family planning services are to be established by December, 2002.

[One hundred and ninety-two] Urban Health Centres that provide mother and child health care services to the urban poor have been established. These centres are established in collaboration with the local NGOs [nongovernmental organizations]. There are also backward area projects operational in Mahabubnagar and RR [Ranga Reddy] districts. We have also improved coverage in tribal areas by positioning 8500 Community Health Workers who assist on both areas of health and family welfare.

To sum up, the wide acceptance of planned parenthood has given the government the impetus to concentrate on improving various other mother and child health services. Having achieved a significant drop in the decadal growth rate, we are now working towards improving the overall health and well being of the families in the State.

"Instead of diverting resources toward population control, governments . . . should support open immigration and policies that promote economic growth."

Governments Should Not Promote Population Control

Christopher Lingle

Christopher Lingle argues in the following viewpoint that government promotion of population control is misguided. He insists that every human being added to a country's population adds economic value by producing goods. He maintains further that the insistence of developed countries (which consist mainly of whites) that developing nations (which consist mainly of nonwhites) limit their populations is implicitly racist in nature. Lingle concludes that rather than encouraging population control, governments should concentrate on promoting economic growth. Christopher Lingle is a professor of economics at Universidad Francisco Marrooquin in Guatemala.

As you read, consider the following questions:

1. In the author's opinion, why are population planners and reproductive-rights advocates dismayed about U.S. funding cuts to the UNFPA?
2. To what two factors does Christopher Lingle attribute the quadrupling of the earth's population in the last century?
3. What does the author argue is the internal check to excessive population growth?

Once again the Bush administration has come under fire for a decision that runs counter to conventional wisdom. Undeterred by widespread denunciations after opposing the Kyoto Protocol,[1] it announced that funds appropriated by Congress to the United Nations Population Fund (UNFPA) would be cut back. With all the hue and cry about the dangers of population growth in the world, it would seem that an agency that supports reproductive health in developing countries should be a sacred cow. Even so, it is fair to ask whether this indicates a sort of bullheadness or insensitivity on the part of the President [George W. Bush] and his team or whether many of the shapers of world opinion have their facts wrong.

Unfortunately, this issue has become wrapped up with the abortion controversy. Both sides have sought to occupy the moral high ground. For its part, the Bush administration points to the use of UNFPA funds to support compulsory abortions in China. This should be uncontroversial to anyone outside the policy-making corridors of Beijing. It beggars the imagination that pro-choice advocates would support the use of force to require abortions, contraception, or sterilization.

Population Increases Offer Gains

From their side, population planners and reproductive-rights advocates insist that cutting funds will harm the interests of many women, especially in developing countries. Funding cuts are paired with horrific images of millions of unwanted pregnancies, related medical complications, and an unabated spread of AIDS.

The Bush administration might have found itself on more tenable ground if it shifted the debate toward the persistent negative image associated with population increases per se. For herein lies a truly prickly question. Neglected in this debate is that having more human beings actually constitutes a net gain. Instead, supporters of population planning (both voluntary or involuntary) start with the assumption that there

1. In 1997 more than 160 countries met in Kyoto, Japan, to negotiate binding limitations on greenhouse gas emissions for developed nations. The United States did not sign the protocol.

are already too many of us on our fair earth. And there is surprisingly little dissent to this view. Sharp declines in infant mortality and improved health care have increased life spans and contributed to the population's nearly quadrupling within a century, from around 1.6 billion in 1900 to almost 6 billion in 2000. Worries about a global population explosion brought warnings of worldwide famine and immiseration. Happily, these predictions have not been borne out. One eloquent body of work that should be more widely heeded is that of the late economist Julian Simon, who had a remarkably undismal view of the world. His optimism is best expressed in his book *The Ultimate Resource*. Therein, he identifies human beings as being capable of resolving most problems that confront us.

Ignoring the view of thinkers like Simon, political leaders in both India and China were caught in the trap of a negative logic that allowed abusive acts against their citizens in the name of "sound" public policy. Clearly, the forced sterilization and abortions they pursued were a violation of the most basic principles of human dignity. Their actions reflect a disregard for the value-added potential that is inherent in each and every human being. Yet they are obviously not alone. Even conventional economic data calculation reflects a negative bias against population growth.

Implicit Racism

Consider the calculation of per capita income whereby national income is divided by the size of the population. This means that an additional person will increase the denominator and reflect a decrease in the material well-being of a community. However, a batch of new puppies born to a breeder will increase the numerator and reflect an enhancement in economic conditions. Such an anomaly comes from ignoring the imputed present value of the future flow of benefits from a newly born human.

Despite their likely denials of such, there is an implicit racism in the demands of population-control advocates. Since many Western developed countries have shrinking populations, insistence on limiting population growth involves holding back the numbers of black, brown, and yellow peoples.

Although considerable evidence refutes the dismal view of population growth, it persists. Consider the fact that the areas of highest population density are the most prosperous and often the most hospitable. Amsterdam, Hong Kong,

Overpopulation Is Not the Problem

The world's problem is not too many people, but lack of political and economic freedom. Powerful evidence comes from pairs of countries that had the same culture and history and much the same standard of living when they split apart after World War II—East and West Germany, North and South Korea, Taiwan and China. In each case the centrally planned communist country began with less population "pressure", as measured by density per square kilometer, than did the market-directed economy. And the communist and non-communist countries also started with much the same birth rates. But the market-directed economies performed much better economically than the centrally-planned economies. This powerful demonstration cuts the ground from under population growth as a likely explanation of poor economic performance. . . .

The most important benefit of population size and growth is the increase it brings to the stock of useful knowledge. Minds matter economically as much as, or more than, hands or mouths. Progress is limited largely by the availability of trained workers.

In the long run the basic forces influencing the state of humanity and its progress are a) the number of people who are alive to consume, but also to produce goods and knowledge; and b) the level of wealth. Those are the great variables which control the advance of civilization. . . .

In 1986, the National Research Council and the National Academy of Sciences published a monograph on population growth and economic development prepared by a prestigious scholarly group. This "official" report reversed almost completely the frightening conclusions of the previous 1971 NAS report. "The scarcity of exhaustible resources is at most a minor constraint on economic growth", it said. It found that additional people bring benefits as well as costs. Even the World Bank, for many years a major institutional purveyor of gloom-and-doom notions about population growth, reported in 1984 that the world's natural resource situation provides no reason to limit population growth.

Julian Simon, *The Ultimate Resource II*, 1998.

London, Singapore, and Tokyo are prime examples of this. And even though Bombay and Cairo are heavily polluted, they are both certainly more prosperous and productive than the surrounding countryside.

Interestingly, advocates of population control are subject to strong personal incentives to exaggerate the dangers. Concocting horrific images of overpopulation allows politicians to lay claim to more resources from taxpayers (whose numbers they paradoxically wish to see increase!). Similarly, "nongovernmental organizations" (NGOs) stand to gain funds by beating the same drum.

Internal Checks

It turns out that population growth has internal checks. For example, people who are richer, healthier, and better educated tend to have smaller families. According to U.N. estimates, there will be little growth in the world's population growth after 2100 and the population will be stable at just below 11 billion. This is because the population growth rate peaked at about 2 percent a year in the early 1960s and has been declining ever since. It is now 1.26 percent and is expected to fall to 0.46 percent in 2050. Countries where fertility rates are at sub-replacement levels constitute about 44 percent of the world's total population and include many developing countries. On the one hand, high rates of economic development along with rising per capita income has heralded a declining pace of population growth due to rapid decreases in birthrates. On the other hand, it is troubling counterpoint that countries with lower levels of economic development are experiencing a discernible decline in life spans.

Many countries have population profiles that show increased aging. With progressive improvement in life expectancies and health conditions during long intervals of peace, the median age of many populations has increased. With more individuals able to better their lives, it can be said that the overall human condition has improved.

There are other ways to cope with local population growth. One of the simplest would be to allow more open immigration. However, populists mount opposition by invoking the fear of infiltration by terrorist organizations or the dilution of indigenous culture. These claims find eager support among trade unionists who want to keep out other workers who seek to improve their lot. Looking at it from a purely economic standpoint, there is considerable evidence that migration yields net benefits to receiving countries. Incoming migrants tend to be younger and healthier than the receiving population. And their choice to move away from the familiarities of their home country implies a high initiative to work. In all events, most economic migrants take up jobs that locals are unwilling or unable to fill.

Increase Economic Growth

The other way to offset the pressures of the peopling of the earth is to take steps to allow higher economic growth. There are various benefits from this. First, increases in average income tend to lead to declining birth rates. Second, higher levels of income provide both the desire and the means to solve a wide range of problems.

The perceived problems of global population growth are failures of governance. Instead of diverting resources toward population control, governments and NGOs should support open immigration and policies that promote economic growth.

"It seems unlikely populations could be reduced rapidly without some coercive measures."

Aggressive Population Control Policies Should Be Supported

Carol A. Kates

Carol A. Kates argues in the following viewpoint that governments should use aggressive, coercive methods of birth control to rapidly reduce their populations to sustainable levels. She insists that individuals cannot be depended upon to make voluntary, rational birth control decisions, and that the government should establish population programs that limit family size. Kates maintains that empowering and educating women, while beneficial, is not the fastest or most effective method of population reduction. Carol A. Kates is a professor of philosophy at Ithaca College in Ithaca, New York.

As you read, consider the following questions:
1. What does the author argue is the solution to the "tragedy of the commons"?
2. In the author's opinion, why do some economists reject coercive methods of population control even though they are effective?
3. In addition to the Cairo agenda, what does Carol A. Kates insist is responsible for diminished international support for population programs?

While scientists debate the precise carrying capacity of the planet, the accelerating risk of ecosystem collapse urgently requires our species to resolve a dilemma which Garrett Hardin called "the tragedy of the commons". The environment, with its ultimately limited resources of land, clean air and water, food, and so on, is treated as a 'commons' when it is viewed as an unpriced asset which may be freely used by all. The inevitable result of this *laissez-faire* approach is the eventual exhaustion of shared resources, as each individual acts to maximize his gain. Hardin applied this analysis to population ("freedom to [over] breed"), though it is easily generalized to include a system of production and consumption which in a similar way exploits the environment as a "free good." The solution is an enforceable rational agreement to regulate the commons, that is, "mutual coercion mutually agreed upon" to limit reproduction and, by extension, the unsustainable use of environmental resources in production and consumption.

Impose Coercive Limits on Reproductive Liberty

Reducing population to a sustainable level (at some desirable level of consumption), would obviously require a major global effort, not merely to subsidize and distribute effective modern contraceptives, but to offer incentives and impose penalties to influence fertility, manipulate institutional variables, aggressively counter pronatalist cultural values, and, very likely, impose coercive limits on reproductive liberty. However, some or all of those measures have been strongly opposed by many religious conservatives and by an influential bloc of left-liberal and feminist advocates of 'reproductive liberty'. The contentious 1994 UN [United Nations] International Conference on Population and Development [UNICPD] in Cairo declared reproductive liberty to be a human right, and shifted the focus of development efforts from population programs to women's reproductive health. In this political climate, it is perhaps not surprising that the September 2002 U.N. World Summit on Sustainable Development produced a long list of proposals to achieve sustainable economic growth without a single mention of sustainable population *levels*. . . .

Probably the most common argument made by liberals who acknowledge "demographic problems" is the claim that a crisis is not yet imminent, and therefore the overpopulation threat can be effectively addressed through economic development and especially through better educational and economic opportunities for women, rather than by resorting to methods which violate "human rights".

For those who believe there *is* an imminent crisis, the question is whether the voluntary decisions of rational and "empowered" individuals can be relied upon to resolve the problem in time, or whether governments should establish population programs, even coercive ones, to achieve ecological sustainability.

Demographic Transition Model

Confidence in economic development as a solution to demographic problems was originally based on the so-called demographic transition model, which has been influential since the 1940s. This theory explains reductions in fertility rates as a function of economic development, prosperity, education, and reduced infant mortality. However, this model has failed to explain recent declines in fertility rates in developing countries, forcing demographers to search for more complex theories.

There is evidence that improvements in women's status significantly enhance the transition to lower fertility rates. Women who have access to birth control, and are able to make decisions about reproduction, are likely to have fewer children. So, it might appear that a left/liberal defense of "reproductive liberty" and a feminist perspective on the need to "empower" women through access to education and paid employment coincide with the most efficient means to resolve the population problem. This is exactly the position which has been argued by such influential political economists as Amartya Sen.

Coercive Methods Versus Human Rights

Sen has acknowledged a need to slow down population growth (for environmental reasons), or "the world certainly would be tremendously overcrowded before the end of the twenty-first century". But he rejects coercive methods as incompatible with human rights and as unnecessary, because empowering women is the most efficient way to achieve demographic transition. Sen has repeatedly cited a comparison between fertility reductions in the Indian state of Kerala and in China as evidence for the efficiency claim. Kerala reduced its fertility rate from 3.0 in 1979 to 1.8 in 1991 with no coercive policies, while China, which introduced the one-child policy in 1979, only reduced its rate in that period from 2.8 to 2.0. Sen argues that the key variables which explain fertility reduction in Kerala are high levels of basic education, especially for women, along with access to health care and an important role for women in the economic and political life of Kerala. If this example can be generalized, it follows that coercive population programs are unnecessary. In effect, women's reproductive rights are the best contraceptive.

The first counter-point to Sen is that, although women *are* likely to have smaller families if given the choice, the strength of anti-feminist forces in some parts of the world almost certainly rules out rapid improvements in female status. Sen's discussion of Kerala fails to point out that the "empowerment" of women in Kerala did *not* occur within a short time period. What the Kerala example shows is, not what was done in 12 years, but rather the depth of the social revolution which took place over 200 years through an "activist democracy": the organized power and sacrifice of the poor, aided by some remarkable allies from the upper castes. Kerala is in many ways a region with a uniquely progressive culture and politics, and should certainly not be taken as a model for a realistic near-term global solution to the environmental crisis posed by overpopulation.

Kerala Was Unique

The conditions which made Kerala's rapid decline in fertility possible include some remarkable and beneficial elements in the culture and history of the region. Among other factors, the matrilineal Nair caste (about 16% of the population) had a long tradition of female control over sexuality and property which empowered these women long before modern reforms. A successful grassroots social revolution which began with a rebellion against the caste system starting in the early nineteenth century radicalized the population and laid the foundation for a broad coalition between the lower castes and the trade union and Communist movement which emerged in the 1930's. Kerala has benefitted from redistributive policies carried out since 1957, when the first democratically elected Marxist government in the world assumed office. Starting with a radical land reform passed in 1969, a series of governments have implemented progressive policies, including state pensions for agricultural workers, subsidies for health care, food and other essential items, and a highly effective campaign to achieve "total literacy".

Gable. © 1994 by Globe Interactive, a division of Bell Globemedia Publishing, Inc. Reproduced by permission of *The Globe and Mail*.

The government decided to make population an issue in the 1960s, appealing to the state's "rationalist" tradition to make the case that smaller families were a condition for creating a well-educated, prosperous society. Contraceptives were widely distributed, IUD's inserted for free at local clinics, and women activists spear-headed a grass roots campaign to promote a small family norm. Today, both men and women in Kerala are given a small cash incentive if they choose sterilization, and most women elect sterilization after the second or third child. [R. Franke and B. Chasin] attribute the success of the program to the radical social changes which preceded it: "In Kerala, the determinants came in the right order—a reduction in infant and child mortality, followed by or along with an increase in female education, followed by redistributive policies, and finally the official family-planning programme".

Empowerment Is Not the Most Effective Method

The precondition for these social changes was, again, 200 years of social revolution. Kerala emancipated itself from an especially rigid caste system, religious hatred, gender discrimination, and illiteracy, and the people of the region have made government accountable, demanding massive redistribution and an array of social welfare benefits which are now being tested by the pressures of the global economy.

In the world outside Kerala, it is unlikely that empowering women is the most efficient *general* solution to overpopulation. The point is *not* that empowering women has no effect on fertility, but rather that, contrary to Sen, the time frame for reducing population is probably too short for the cultural evolution, perhaps revolution, needed to accomplish this in some parts of the world. A 1994 UN population and development review found that improvement in women's status since the 1980 Women's Convention (CEDAW) was "much slower than expected" and in fact had deteriorated in many developing countries, and attributed pervasive and continuing gender discrimination to the traditions and practices controlling social relationships. Patriarchal gender norms are often rationalized by religious beliefs and traditions which support high fertility as well as subjugation of women, especially in agrarian societies. . . .

Slowing the Pace of Fertility Decline

A second response to Sen is that the shift from a focus on population to women's empowerment and reproductive health services may actually be one of several factors which will slow the pace of fertility decline in developing countries. One of the prominent themes highlighted in the UN Population Division's 2002 expert group meetings was noticeably reduced support for population programs since Cairo. Jason Finkle questioned the "problematic" result of the Cairo paradigm shift from macro social concerns to individual welfare, suggesting that the exclusive focus on "empowerment of women" had a negative result. . . .

John Caldwell believes the Cairo action program "discouraged many involved in existing family planning programs by seeming to condemn what they had hitherto regarded as past successes and by appearing to ask more than their countries' health services could provide in the foreseeable future. It has almost certainly also confused donors who had not previously considered that the much more expensive national education and health services warranted the same proportional support as did the family planning programs". Steven Sindling noted that: "assistance for population programs has fallen well short of the goals set at [Cairo]. . . . The absence of a sense of urgency about high fertility at senior policy levels, either in donor capitals or in most developing countries, suggests to me that the 'population movement' as it has existed since the 1960s, may be close to having run its course". Reduced funding for population programs is cause for concern, not only because fertility decline has not begun in many countries and is slowing in others, but because [according to Sindling,] "we are in the era of the largest cohort of reproductive aged people in history" and even if all of these people only wanted two children, "the consequences of even small differences in unwanted fertility will . . . be very large".

The Effect of Conservative Religious Opposition

Diminished international support for population programs, including funding for the distribution of subsidized modern contraceptives, cannot be blamed entirely on the Cairo agenda. Conservative religious opposition to contraception and abortion, coupled with a belief that the remedy for poverty is market reform and free trade rather than family planning, account for significantly reduced funding from the U.S. (In 2003, the U.S. donates only 300 million condoms annually, down from about 800 million in 1992.) Further, unexpectedly rapid fertility declines in many developing countries, along with below-replacement level fertility in many developed countries, has created the impression in some quarters that population is "no longer a problem," and indeed, that in rich countries, the "problem" may even be low fertility. In any case, the strange alliance of religious conservatives, feminists, "progressive" liberals, and free market ideologists now poses a threat to the environment and human welfare. John Caldwell points out that the loss of interest in population growth, reflected in changing "attitudes, policies and expenditures," may have a "significant demographic impact", perhaps making the difference between an eventually stable population of 8 billion or one of 12 billion. "The differences in long-term environmental sustainability could be huge".

Increase in Contraception Needed

In the case of Sub-Saharan Africa, a study of proximate (direct) determinants of fertility concluded that a transition to low fertility will require a significant increase in the use of modern contraceptives, and that the "full reproductive health agenda" poses "problems" for the region by undermining a focus on much needed core family planning services. The 2002 UN Population Division's report on demographic transition in intermediate-fertility countries notes that most below-replacement fertility societies have very high levels (65–85%) of use of effective contraceptives, implying that a large increase in contraception will be necessary for fertility reduction in the developing world. John Bongaarts finds some empirical support for human development (especially health and education) as (intermediate) determinants of fertility transition (citing the examples of Sri Lanka and Kerala), but also stresses that replacement-level fertility cannot be achieved without "a high level of birth control. . . . Ready access to family planning methods and abortion services is needed to achieve low levels of unwanted childbearing". A study of Nigeria [by B. Feyisetan and A. Bankole] which cast doubt on the odds of reaching replacement level by 2050 noted: "In almost all the countries that have experienced significant reductions in fertility levels . . . government has demonstrated strong support for fertility control programs. Unfortunately, the same cannot be said of Nigeria now".

Given the fact that about 80% of all contraceptive users receive their supplies from public sector programs, and that it is estimated about 100 million women in all nations (excluding China) have an unmet need for contraception, even as a billion young people between 15 and 24 enter their reproductive years, reduced support for family planning programs is certain to have a major impact on fertility. Thus, the efficiency of the Cairo paradigm as a replacement for population programs is a matter of critical concern.

Government Support Is Important

Fertility reduction has been achieved under a wide, even "bewildering" range of social conditions: when economic conditions have been improving or deteriorating, in societies with both high and low living standards, and in countries with both increasing and decreasing gender inequity. However, it is clear that, whatever the underlying causes may be, strong government support for efficient population programs has produced striking results in many developing countries. . . .

Under the white (apartheid) government of South Africa, fertility declined at an unprecedented rate in the Sub-Saharan region, from a TFR [total fertility rate] of about 6.6 for black Africans in 1960 to 3.1 in 1998. Although the well-funded National Family Planning Programme launched in 1974 was explicitly motivated by demographic and racist fears, and did nothing to improve black African economic welfare or empower women, it was nonetheless embraced by many African women for their own reasons, probably without the knowledge of their spouses. This finding suggests that in patriarchal societies creating incentives for men to reduce fertility would be effective.

Women deserve exactly the same rights as men. However, neither men nor women have an absolute "right" to procreate. If one believes that reducing fertility as rapidly as possible is essential, and if narrowly-focused population programs are in some cases the most efficient means to that goal, it follows that *substituting* a women's rights agenda for effective population measures is, from an environmental perspective, misguided and harmful.

A final objection to the "empowerment" solution to high

fertility is that, if the carrying capacity estimates made by [W.] Rees, [M.] Wackernagel, [D.] Pimentel, and others are correct, reducing human load to a sustainable level will require absolute *reductions* in population, and not merely a transition to replacement level at somewhere between 8 and 12 billion. Even with below-replacement fertility, population reduction would be a slow process. For example, David Pimentel estimates that it would take more than 100 years to achieve an "optimal" global population of 2 billion, even if each couple could be limited to an average 1.5 children. And, since human load is a function of both consumption (and technology) and population size, countries with high consumption levels have the largest ecological deficits, despite generally low birth rates. From this perspective, the U.S., despite the empowerment of women, has been described as the most "overpopulated" country in the world. Yet, it is fair to say that there is currently no broad support in the U.S. for the view that U.S. fertility rates are too high. And while the UN's Environmental Program projects a "sustainability" scenario which requires a sudden turn away from materialism in affluent nations, there is no sign of this so far, and it is very unlikely that rich countries will ever agree to significant redistribution of wealth based on altruism. Global bickering about what is "fair" is likely to produce stalemate. The CIA demographic scenario suggests some level of confidence in government and corporate circles (at least before 9/11/2001), that environmental damage (and its social consequences) can be managed, and that the U.S. and other affluent allies will continue to enjoy material prosperity without reducing population size.

Altruism Is Not the Answer

Although altruism is unlikely to save the environment, there might be some hope based on enlightened self-interest. If, as many predict, environmental problems begin to accelerate, with corresponding damage to human interests, it should become obvious that everyone is harmed by damage to the ecosystem. The U.S. and other rich countries do not have the option of living in "gated communities" on planet Earth. Indeed, we face a bleak future . . . unless each nation agrees to terms which will resolve the tragedy of the global commons. On the face of it, the best, perhaps only, way out of the dilemma is an agreement requiring each nation to eliminate its ecological deficit, making its own trade-off between consumption and population size. No country would be permitted to "live beyond its means" by emigration or by exporting pollution. It is likely that, faced with a choice between population reduction or dramatic reductions in consumption (or other constraints), most people would choose the former. Each nation could choose its method of achieving sustainability. Perhaps in some countries education, the example set by enlightened leaders, and fear of environmental collapse would be sufficient to reach population targets. However, it seems unlikely populations could be reduced rapidly without some coercive measures.

"What . . . proponents of strong measures to control . . . population refuse to acknowledge is that population control policies . . . just do not work."

Aggressive Population Control Policies Should Be Abandoned

Amit Sen Gupta

Aggressive population policies such as female sterilization waste money and do not work, argues Amit Sen Gupta in the following viewpoint. He maintains that birthrates in developing nations such as India will fall naturally and more quickly as child survival rates increase and women become better educated and seek jobs outside the home. Gupta insists that economic development, not aggressive or coercive population control, is the most effective way to reduce developing nations' population. Amit Sen Gupta is a physician with India's Public Health Campaign. He is also treasurer of the Delhi Science Forum, a public interest organization that explores science policy issues.

As you read, consider the following questions:

1. What argument does the author provide to prove the ineffectiveness of female sterilization as a method of population control?
2. To what does Gupta attribute the fall in birthrates in Kerala?
3. In Gupta's opinion, what do the poor in India need?

Amit Sen Gupta, "Lamentations on the Billionth Baby," www.delhiscienceforum.org, May 2000. Copyright © 2000 by Delhi Science Forum. Reproduced by permission.

The arrival of the billionth baby in India has been greeted with the expected responses. International financial institutions, NGOs [nongovernmental organizations], the Indian Government and assorted political parties have seen this as an opportunity to reaffirm their commitment towards population control. The parrot-like mouthing of platitudes regarding the dangers to the nation of a rapidly increasing population reminds one of an old adage—the more things change, the more they remain the same. India's population control programme is arguably the oldest in the world—started shortly after India's Independence. On the balance all it has to show are repeated lamentations on the programme's inability to effectively reduce the rate of population growth in the country. It is a convenient ploy for the ruling classes and their vocal drum-beaters in the media—for in one stroke the bogey of population can be used to explain away all their failures in providing decent conditions of living to a majority of the Indian population.

Population Control Policies Do Not Work

What the proponents of strong measures to control the country's population refuse to acknowledge is that population control policies—as we view them—just do not work. Take the case of female sterilisation—the principal focus of population policy in India for a decade and a half since the late seventies. For all the money pumped into the programme, data shows that an overwhelming majority of women who undergo sterilisation are those who are past their reproductive lives, i.e. they were unlikely to have conceived any more children even if they had not undergone a sterilisation operation. Of course votaries of the Family Planning programme have a convenient contradictory response to such criticisms. On one hand they would point out the successes of the programme—assorted statistics to show that the programme has actually helped in reducing birth rate, and that in the programme's absence India's population would have been much higher. In the same breath they would also argue that birth rates and population growth rates are still unacceptably high, and hence the population policy should be further strengthened!

147

Kerala's Experience

Let us first examine the evidence regarding the programme's "success" in the last four decades. What do we make of the limited success we have achieved in terms of declining birth rates in the country in the last three or four decades? Everybody would like to talk about Kerala as a success story in containing population growth rate. What few, however, are prepared to say is that Kerala never had a very strong population policy. On the contrary states like Haryana (with one of the highest birth rates in the country) have received several national awards for having successfully implemented population programmes. When population policy theorists talk of Kerala, where the low birth rates approximate those of highly developed countries, they seldom (if ever) point out that Kerala was the first state (and still only one of three, including W. Bengal and Tripura) to initiate radical land reform programmes in 1957 under the first left led government in the country. Kerala's fall in birth rates followed a set of major socio-economic advances that led to a fall in infant and child mortality rates, increase in literacy rates (crucially increases in women's literacy rates), etc. The process in Kerala was not duplicated in other parts of the country because of the kind of socio-economic policies that were followed by the Indian government. Yet, some advances were made in most states. These advances were, in part, a result of the needs of the ruling classes (viz. an increase in education and health infrastructure) and in significant measure wrested from the ruling classes by numerous struggles of the working people in the country. Whatever the genesis, these advances, while not matching the needs of India's working people, have led to demonstrable gains in some areas. Thus life expectancy has almost doubled since Independence, infant and child mortality rates have been halved, and literacy rates have increased significantly. There is no evidence that shows that the slowing down of population growth rate in the country has been because of the population policy. In fact Kerala's story would indicate that it has happened in spite of our population policies. Even in the rest of the country, the limited success in containing population can arguably be linked to the limited development in different socio-economic spheres.

History of Population Change

It is important to understand that India's experience regarding population growth is, by no means, unique. All over the globe population increased as a response to economic development. This is most clearly demonstrable under Capitalism, where a major rise in population was seen after the Industrial revolution in the late eighteenth century. Much of this growth was first seen in Europe, the seat of Capitalism as well as that of the concomitant economic development in that period. There are many reasons why this happens. To start with economic development leads to greater availability of food, which in turn leads to higher survival rates. Gradually improved conditions of housing, other civic amenities, improvements in public health infrastructure, education, etc. leads to declining death rates. These conditions also facilitate increase in birth rates—better nutrition enhances the ability of women to bear children, and higher survival rates mean that there are more women who survive through the child bearing age. A combination of high birth rates and high survival rates, thus, provide a dual push to population growth rates. We can thus see a peaking of population growth rates in Europe in the first part of the twentieth century. Let us not forget that England is still twice as densely populated as India, even today.

Birth Rate Declines Depend on Child Survival Rates

The fall in birth rates starts somewhere in the middle of this process of increasing growth rates of population. This happens because the fall in birth rates, initially, is still much slower than the fall in death rates. So, even though less children are born, the population still continues to increase as even less people die. It takes much longer for birth rates to fall to a level where they compensate for the very low death rates. We can see this happening in the developed Capitalist world—Europe, N. America, Japan, etc.—only in the second half of the twentieth century. Decline in birth rates are predicated on a complex set of factors. Crucial to this is child survival rates. In situations where child survival rates are very low, birth rates are high because families produce more children as an "insurance" that at least a few of them will survive up to adulthood.

Increasing Resistance

The old focus on restraining population growth grew out of widespread concern that the unprecedented pace and volume of population growth after 1950 was a serious threat to economic development, public health, and the environment. Many governments supported family planning programs to reduce their birth rate and slow population growth. But national policies intent on "population control" met with increasing resistance and diminishing support by the mid-1990s. Women's health advocates in particular saw (and still see) these policies as infringing on women's basic rights to decide whether and when to have children.

Population Bulletin, March 2001.

The second crucial factor is related to women's position in society and the economy. The old feudal values, where women are seen as just "home-makers" ensure that child rearing remains a full-time occupation for women in the child bearing age. Improved nutrition ensures that the span during which women can produce children increases significantly. Thus women, for 20–25 years move from one pregnancy to the next through much of this period. This cycle is dented only when women start entering the job market to take up independent careers, and are not seen as mere "tubes for producing babies". The cycle is further dented when women are able to independently articulate the need to limit families, as repeated child-births (and early child-birth) take a toll on their health. Moreover, in developed Capitalist societies, the frenetic pursuit of material comforts act as a brake on family size—as a large family compromises access to an array of consumer goods. A combination of these factors has led to precipitate falls in birth rates in much of the developed world, and we see a reverse of the earlier process—birth rates dipping below the low death rates, leading to an actual fall in population.

Passing on the Burden of Guilt

What has been recounted above can be termed as the "natural history" of the dynamics of population change. India is in the kind of situation where Europe was in the first part of the twentieth century—high birth rates and declining death rates leading to an aggregate growth in population. Many of the factors that promote high birth rates—high infant and child mortality, gender discrimination, etc.—are still prevalent in significant measure in most parts of the country. Of particular significance is the severity of gender discrimination, and consequent preference for male children, still prevalent in India. A population policy which does not address these determinants of high birth rates cannot hope to succeed. If we critically examine the so-called successes of the population policy in this country, it should be evident that these have taken place not because of the population policies pursued in India, but because of limited progress made in social and economic development—however halting, inadequate and iniquitous they may have been. So the prescription should be one of rejecting the present paradigm that determines population policies in the country, and not one of further strengthening such policies.

When international "development" agencies, foreign funded NGOs and assorted socialites and celebrities speak tearfully of the poor Indians who need to adopt family planning, they essentially seek to pass on the burden of the effects of undiminished exploitation by their own class onto millions of poor Indians. India's population continues to rise because a majority of Indians are poor, denied of basic health and education facilities, and without sustainable forms of employment. We do not need a population policy that targets the poor, and especially women amongst them. The poor in this country need access to methods by which they can limit their families. But for them to be able to do so they need a much larger set of enabling conditions. To deny them these conditions and simultaneously to seek to pass on the burden of guilt for India's slow pace of development amounts to making a mockery of their present pathetic conditions of living.

"It is necessary to continue the present family planning policy . . . in implementing population and family planning program[s]."

China's One-Child Policy Should Be Continued

Information Office of the State Council of the People's Republic of China

China's one-child policy has proven to be a successful method of population control for the past thirty years and therefore should be continued, argues the Information Office of the State Council of the People's Republic of China in the following viewpoint. The office maintains that the one-child policy meets the unique needs of the nation, which has a huge population, inadequate resources, and low levels of scientific and economic development. The Information Office of the State Council of the People's Republic of China is responsible for releasing information from the government to the people of China and the international community.

As you read, consider the following questions:

1. According to the authors, what practices—in addition to one couple, one child—does the Chinese government encourage to control population?
2. What will be the annual net increase in China's population in the next decade, according to the authors?
3. Where should family planning priorities be placed so that balanced regional development can be realized, in the authors' opinion?

Information Office of the State Council of the People's Republic of China, "China's Population and Development in the Twenty-First Century," www.cpirc. org.cn, 2000. Copyright © 2000 by the China Population Information and Research Center. Reproduced by permission.

The 21st century [has arrived]. With the rapid development of science and technology and the swift changes in the world economic order and patterns, population and development have become an increasingly important issue, which draws broad concern of the international community. It is the common choice of all countries to seek a way to achieve sustainable development with population, economy, society, resources and environment all in harmony.

China is a developing country with the biggest population in the world. A sample survey shows that China's population had reached 1.26 billion by the end of 1999 (excluding the population of the Hong Kong and Macao Special Administrative Regions and Taiwan Province), accounting for about 21% of the world total. In order to better understand the pattern and trend of the population change, further rein in population growth, improve population quality, and properly formulate a population policy and social and economic development plan for the 21st century, the Chinese Government conducted its fifth national census in November 2000. The result will be published once all data are processed.

Population Restricts Development

China has a huge population, but a weak economic foundation with relatively inadequate per-capita resources. These are its basic national conditions. Many contradictions and problems in China's economic and social development are closely associated with the issue of population, which has become the key factor and primary problem restricting China's economic and social development. Whether the population problem can be properly solved has direct bearing on the improvement of the population quality and the living standards of the Chinese people, as well as the prosperity of the Chinese nation. It also concerns the world peace and development.

In line with the strategic goal of the nation's modernization drive and proceeding from national conditions, the Chinese Government has formulated and implemented a population policy which conforms to China's reality and has greatly contributed to the stabilization of the national and the world population and to the promotion of human development and progress.

The Chinese Government is willing to continue its efforts together with the international community to effectively solve the problem of population and development. The Chinese Government firmly believes that China's population and development cause will develop further in the 21st century and that China will make still greater contribution to the civilization and progress of mankind.

Since the 1970s, especially since the initiation of the reform and opening-up drive, China has formulated a basic state policy to promote family planning in an all-round way so as to slow down population growth and improve population quality in terms of health and education. The Government encourages late marriage and late childbearing, and advocates the practice of "one couple, one child" and of "having a second child with proper spacing in accordance with the laws and regulations." Family planning is also advocated among the ethnic minorities. Various provinces, autonomous regions and municipalities directly under the Central Government have formulated their own policies and regulations according to local conditions.

China's Population Program Is Successful

The Chinese Government pays great attention to the issue of population and development and has placed it on the agenda as an important part in the overall plan of China's national economic and social development. The Government consistently emphasizes that population growth should be compatible with socio-economic development and be in concert with resource utilization and environmental protection. Since the 1990s, the Central Government has convened a National Summit Meeting on the issue of population and development once a year for the sake of adopting important decisions and measures based upon discussion and analysis of the major problems. The Government organizes and coordinates the relevant departments and mass organizations to implement the population and family planning program, striving to integrate the family planning program with economic development, poverty eradication, protection of ecological environment, rational resource utilization, universal education, advancement of public health and social security, and improvement of women's status. This is aimed at seeking a thorough solution to the problem of population and development.

After nearly 30 years of efforts, China has found a successful way of dealing with the population issue in a comprehensive manner, a path suited to the country's unique conditions. A system of regulating and adjusting population growth with a proper management mechanism of the family planning program has gradually come into being. This is a system in keeping with the demands of the market economy. China's population and development program has achieved universally acknowledged success. The citizens' rights to subsistence and development and their rights in the socio-economic and cultural fields have been notably improved. . . .

Population Control Is Beneficial

The whole society has gained a better understanding of the issue of population. It is agreed that population control is beneficial to a coordinated and sustainable development of population, economy, society, resources and environment; birth control should be stepped up and a laissez-faire attitude should be guarded against; while slowing down population growth, efforts should be made to improve the population quality, reproductive health, quality of life and well being in general so as to realize human development in an all-round way; the issue of population is essentially a problem of development and could only be solved through economic, social and cultural development. The same period saw impressive changes in the people's attitude towards marriage, childbearing and the elderly support. The traditional concepts of "early marriage, early childbirth", "the more sons, the more happiness" and "men are superior to women" have been gradually replaced by the scientific and advanced concepts of "late marriage, and later childbearing, fewer and healthier births" and "boys and girls are equal". More and more people have voluntarily practiced family planning. The first marriage age for women of childbearing age averaged 23.57 years in 1998, as against 20.8 years in 1970. The contraceptive prevalence rate of married women of childbearing age reached 83%, and the average family size had decreased

Major Figures of Population and Family Planning (1994–2000)

Item	Unit	1994	1995	1996	1997	1998	1999	2000
Total Population	10,000	119850	121121	122389	123626	124810	125909	126583
Birth Rate	‰	17.70	17.12	16.98	16.57	16.03	15.23	
Death Rate	‰	6.49	6.57	6.56	6.51	6.50	6.46	
Natural Growth Rate	‰	11.21	10.55	10.42	10.06	9.53	8.77	
Total Number of Birth	10,000	2104	2063	2067	2038	1991	1909	
Number of Women at Childbearing Ages	100 Million	3.26	3.30	3.33	3.37	3.40	3.45	3.48
Number of Married Women at Childbearing Ages	100 Million	2.3	2.37	2.39	2.43	2.45	2.49	2.51
Percentage of Late Marriage	%	58.5	58.9	59.36	59.31	60.12	60.12	58.99
CPR of Married Women at Childbearing Ages	%	90.7	90.4	91.1	83.8			
Family Planning Acceptors	Million	20895	21412	21817	22101	22245	22559	22683
Contraceptive Methods								
Vasectomy	%	10.9	10.6	10.2	9.2	9.6	9.2	8.9
Female Sterilization	%	40.2	39.9	39.5	40	38.7	38.2	37.6
IUD	%	40.7	41.7	42.5	43.4	44.5	45.5	46.3
Implant	%	0.2	0.3	0.4	0.5	0.4	0.4	0.4
Pill	%	3.2	2.9	2.8	2.1	2.4	2.2	2.1
Condom	%	3.8	3.8	3.8	4.0	3.8	3.9	4.2
Spermicide	%	0.6	0.5	0.5	0.2	0.4	0.3	0.3
Others	%	0.4	0.3	0.3	0.6	0.2	0.2	0.2

Source: National Bureau of Statistics, People's Republic of China, May 14, 2002.

from 4.84 members in 1971 to 3.63 members in 1998. . . .

The Chinese Government knows clearly that the contradiction between population and development in China remains acute, and that there still exist many difficulties and challenges: the population growth will continue for a prolonged period of time, with an annual net increase of over 10 million in the next decade or so, which will exert great pressure on economy, society, resources, environment and the sustained development as a whole; it is difficult to change entirely the relatively low-level population quality in a short time, which is incompatible with the rapid development of science and technology; the sharp increase of labor force has placed great pressure upon the job market; the arrival of an aged society with a relatively under-developed economy has made it more difficult to establish a comprehensive social security system; with the unbalanced economic and social development among different regions continuing to exist for a long period, it is a most arduous task to eradicate poverty; the increase of floating population, peasants entering towns and cities and population redistribution in different areas will exert impact on the traditional economic and social management system as well as the relevant population policies; in the process of improving the socialist market economic system, various contradictions and problems will emerge, and the complexity of the issue of population and development will remain the same.

China Follows Its Own Path

Taking into consideration its basic national conditions, including a big population, inadequate per-capita resources and a low level of economic and scientific development, China would persistently follow its own path in tackling the issue of population and development. It would draw on other countries' managerial expertise and scientific achievement and tackle its own population and development issue in accordance with its own specific conditions. China would persistently follow its sustainable development strategy and bring about a coordinated development of population, economy, society, resources and environment so as to realize national modernization with comprehensive human development. It would combine the universal principle of human rights with its national conditions, give top priority to the rights to subsistence and development, and facilitate the people's enjoyment of a higher standard of basic rights and freedom in civil, political, economic, social and cultural areas. China respects different cultural background, religious beliefs, and moral concepts. Taking into full consideration the unity between priorities and conditions, rights and obligations, China has formulated and implemented population and development plans and policies to ensure that all social members enjoy an equal opportunity for development. . . .

Emphasis on Contraception and Services

In order to keep a low fertility level, it is necessary to continue the present family planning policy and follow the effective working principles in implementing population and family planning program[s]. The population regulation and management system should be introduced in line with the socialist market economy. The grassroots work should be intensified and favorable conditions actively created so that the population and family planning program can be integrated with the community management system and the comprehensive service network. Priorities should be given to the family planning program in the central and western rural areas so that a balanced regional development can be realized. It is also necessary to reform and improve the population management system of the program objectives, so that the way of thinking and the working style with regard to the family planning program can be improved.

Quality services should be greatly promoted. Emphasis should be put on information, education, communication, contraception and regular services. It is necessary to disseminate knowledge on science and offer quality services to people in their daily life and childbearing matters, so as to meet their needs in family planning and reproductive health, thus promoting human development in a comprehensive way.

"Despite over three decades of reports in the West of the crimes of the one-child policy, very little is being done."

China's One-Child Policy Should Be Ended

Society for the Protection of Unborn Children

The Society for the Protection of Unborn Children argues in the following viewpoint that China's one-child policy is morally abhorrent because it advocates the use of forced abortion and sterilization, infanticide, and the deliberate killing of orphans through neglect. Further, the society claims that Western governments and population control agencies are in collusion with the Chinese government in implementing the policy, and that only pro-life advocacy groups are willing to speak out against the atrocities. The Society for the Protection of Unborn Children is a British pro-life advocacy group.

As you read, consider the following questions:

1. According to the Society for the Protection of Unborn Children, how does the Chinese government enforce its one-child policy?
2. What is the true purpose of the Law on Population and Birth Planning, in the authors' opinion?
3. What do the authors argue British people should do to help end China's one-child policy?

China's one-child policy has recently been described [by Wendy McElroy] as "arguably the greatest bioethical atrocity on the globe." Since the 1970s, the Chinese government has conducted a programme of population control through forced abortion, infanticide, forced sterilisation, forced use of abortifacient birth control, abandonment of children and deliberate killing of orphans through neglect. The programme is enforced through severe penalties for those who do not comply with the policy, including extortionate fines, destruction of property, imprisonment and even torture.

Little Protest from the West

Despite over three decades of reports in the West of the crimes of the one-child policy, very little is being done by governments and human rights organisations about the policy. This is partly because the policy's victims are mainly the unborn, whom the Western world largely neglect, but also partly because many Western governments and wealthy population control agencies support the policy in various ways. Most of the opposition to the policy has come from pro-life organizations like SPUC [Society for the Protection of Unborn Children]. SPUC has in recent years taken a leading role on the issue, working closely with expert groups, in particular the Population Research Institute (PRI) and the Catholic Family & Human Rights Institute (C-FAM). Prolifers are therefore urged to help support the work of this international pro-life coalition against the one-child policy by lobbying politicians, governments and human rights groups.

In 1979 Chinese Vice-Premier Chen Muhua described the one-child policy saying: "A policy of encouragement and punishment for maternity, with encouragement as the main feature, will be implemented. Parents having one child will be encouraged, and strict measures will be enforced to control the birth of two or more babies. Everything should be done to insure that the natural population growth rate in China falls to zero by 2000."

It has been calculated that between 1971 and 1985 alone there were some 100 million coercive birth-control "operations" in China, including forced sterilisations and forced abortions. In 1983 a massive campaign of compulsory birth control surgeries was carried out, which reportedly produced 14 million abortions, 21 million sterilisations and 18 million IUD [interuterine device] insertions. This campaign was directed by the then minister-in-charge of the State Family Planning Commission (SFPC), Qian Xinzhong.

The One-Child Policy Is Unnecessary

Gu Baochang [a Chinese family-planning expert with the New York–based] Population Council, said he and other experts have begun the process of making an overall case to the government that the one-child policy should be replaced with other comprehensive, voluntary family planning programs. The most likely candidate would be a version of a program now being experimented with across the country that tries to treat family planning as a service provided to customers.

But the entire topic is too sensitive to address in direct discussions with officials because they fear that if the one-child policy were relaxed, it would trigger another population boom. Gu said the government has been told that experts want to study alternatives to the one-child regulation, and because no one has stopped them, they assume the government has given tacit approval.

"We think it's time," said Gu, who also works for a government think tank in Beijing. "So we have a small group now working quietly. Family planning is necessary. Population control is necessary. But it doesn't mean the one-child policy is necessary."

Michael A. Lev, *Chicago Tribune*, April 30, 2000.

In September 2002, the Chinese regime passed the Law on Population and Birth Planning. Misleading claims about the law are being put forward by defenders of the one-child policy, but the law's true purpose is to "uphold a single-child policy for married couples" (article 18; note that unmarried people are not permitted to have children) and to legitimise coercion by reclassifying it as law enforcement. Defenders of the policy also claim that coercive practices are simply "abuses". Rather, the new law is clear that coercion is integral to the policy: family planning minister Zhao Bingli warned that "from the date that the law took effect, those who have an extra-policy birth must face the music.". . .

Ending the One-Child Policy

Write to your MP [Member of Parliament]:

- Informing him/her that China's one-child policy has been made even worse by a new law passed in September 2002.
- Asking him/her to write to the Foreign Office, the Department for International Development, Amnesty International and the Chinese embassy to ask them what they are doing to end the one-child policy. . . .

Write to the House of Commons Foreign Affairs Committee:

- Informing it that China's one-child policy has been strengthened by a new law passed in September 2002.
- Asking it to hold an inquiry into the one-child policy. . . .

Write to Amnesty International UK:

- Asking what Amnesty International is doing to end the one-child policy.
- Expressing disappointment that its 2003 annual report does not mention the one-child policy.
- Asking them why the use of torture and ill-treatment by birth control officials was included in its 2002 annual report but not in the 2003 annual report.
- Asking them to raise China's one-child policy in next year's annual report. . . .

Write to the Chinese embassy:

- Protesting at the Chinese regime's denial of the right to life of unborn children, its neglect of new-born children and its violations of the human rights of couples.
- Telling them that the Chinese regime's attempt to whitewash its new population control law have been exposed in the West.
- Informing them that you will continue to protest against the one-child policy until it is abolished.

"Human-rights activists in the U.S. and Peru have charged [the United Nations Population Fund] with complicity in the coerced sterilization of native Peruvians."

The United States Is Justified in Withdrawing Funds from United Nations' Population Control Programs

Austin Ruse and Douglas A. Sylva

Austin Ruse and Douglas A. Sylva argue in the following viewpoint that the United States is justified in withholding funds from the United Nations Population Fund (UNFPA) because it promotes abortion. They assert that the UNFPA works in collusion with the Chinese government to promote coerced abortion programs as part of China's one-child policy. Austin Ruse is president and Douglas A. Sylva is director of research at the Catholic Family and Human Rights Institute, a nongovernmental organization that monitors UN activity.

As you read, consider the following questions:
1. According to Austin Ruse and Douglas A. Sylva, what UN agency refutes the UNFPA report?
2. How does the UNFPA hope to use its report, in the authors' opinion?
3. What do the authors argue the UNFPA does with the finding it receives from the governments of developed countries such as the United States?

Austin Ruse and Douglas A. Sylva, "Are People the Problem?" *National Review Online*, November 20, 2001. Copyright © 2001 by National Review, Inc., 215 Lexington Ave., New York, NY 10016. Reproduced by permission.

The United Nations Population Fund (UNFPA) gave the world a little glimpse of wedded bliss, U.N.-style, in the population report it released last week [mid-November 2001]. The report describes how in Niger, "Many women now work alongside their husbands scooping salt from pits—something not possible a generation ago." In the whole world, this seemed to be the only good news UNFPA could find (wait until they discover that salt mines have glass ceilings).

Leaving African women's newfound right to backbreaking, perilous labor aside, UNFPA considers the rest of the world in almost irreparable straits. UNFPA, which is in charge of U.N. programs for population control, asserts that as a result of uncontrolled population growth, billions of people are poor and hungry. They also fully expect just about every animal species to be skinned, gobbled, or stuffed into extinction by the great hordes of humanity. The report, entitled "Footprints and Milestones," advances the increasingly discredited population-bomb theory everyone under 40 learned practically at their mother's breast.

The Population Division Disputes the UNFPA Report

The problem with the UNFPA report, however, is that it is flatly contradicted by a more credible U.N. source—the Population Division, the official U.N. number crunchers. The differences between the two reports were so stark and so embarrassing that Population Division chief Joseph Chamie announced that UNFPA's report amounted to little more than propaganda. "The relationship between population and the environment is very complex," he said. "UNFPA is a fund; they have an agenda."

UNFPA claims that population growth has led to intractable poverty, and that "poverty persists and, in many parts of the world, deepens." The Population Division disagrees. "From 1900 to 2000, world population grew from 1.6 billion persons to 6.1 billion. However, while the world population increased close to 4 times, world real gross domestic output increased 20 to 40 times, allowing the world to not only sustain a four-fold population increase, but also to do so at vastly higher standards of living." The Population Division adds that ". . . even many low-income countries have achieved substantial improvements in the quality and length of life."

According to UNFPA, "In many countries population growth has raced ahead of food production," and as a result "some 800 million people are chronically malnourished and 2 billion people lack food security." The Population Division, by contrast, contends that "Over the period 1961–1998 world per capita food available for human consumption increased by 24 per cent, and there is enough being produced for everyone on the planet to be adequately nourished."

Developed Countries Fund the UNFPA

It's highly enjoyable to watch U.N. bureaucrats publicly attack their colleagues' credibility, and UNFPA is an awfully tasty target. But the disagreement also has profound implications. UNFPA hopes to use its new report as proof that "reproductive health" must be financed by the international community. And UNFPA has powerful allies on Capitol Hill.

U.S. funding for UNFPA may rise from last year's level of $21.5 to at least $34 million. If the Democrats in the conference committee (which is now taking place) have their way, funding will go even higher, reaching $37.5 million.[1] Because of governments like our own, UNFPA is backed up by loads of cash, which it uses to bribe developing countries into accepting the UNFPA population theory—and the programs that inevitably follow in its wake. The Population Division, by contrast, has no such cash, only facts.

But UNFPA's credibility is slipping. Its connivance in Chinese population coercion is now an established fact. A number of UNFPA officials have been quoted as praising China's one-child policy. "For all of the bad press, China has achieved the impossible," said the UNFPA representative in Beijing. "The country has solved its population problem." Human-rights activists in the U.S. and Peru have charged UNFPA with complicity in the coerced sterilization of native Peruvians. And new allegations surfaced three weeks ago when eyewitnesses told Representative Henry Hyde's House International Affairs Committee that, despite UNFPA assurances

1. The Bush administration withheld $34 million from the UNFPA in 2002.

to the contrary, forced abortions still occur in UNFPA-funded Chinese counties.

Rejection of Funding Is Correct

Steven Mosher, the president of the Population Research Institute said that, by refusing to allow the UNFPA funds, "the [House Appropriations] Committee in effect criticized China's forced abortion regime and the organization that supports it.". . .

"The committee was right to reject [the funding]," Mosher concluded. "Why should the U.S. abandon its human rights principles to support an organization that refuses to withdraw from a program of forced abortion?"

Steven Ertelt, www.lifenews.com, July 10, 2004.

On the other hand, the Population Division began a drumbeat in 1997 to the effect that, far from facing a population explosion, the world risks a population implosion, and a demographic shift with truly catastrophic consequences. Indeed, in the past three years the Population Division has hosted two expert group meetings at U.N. headquarters where demographic experts from all over the world have agreed that the current downward fertility trajectory will bring about population decline, intergenerational financial warfare, and a pension and health system meltdown. They concluded that, without massive immigration, the developed world faces a future of economic crisis.

The UNFPA Tries to Advance the Spread of Abortion

UNFPA is looking to use the threats of environmental degradation, poverty, sickness, etc., to advance the spread of its favorite things: contraception, sterilization, and abortion. UNFPA's tired argument is that people are the problem, and so the fewer of them, the better. UNFPA is therefore ideologically unprepared to recognize the gravity of the real population problem—fertility decline in the developed world—let alone to address it. Since UNFPA guides the U.N. on population issues, we shouldn't be surprised if the U.N. keeps handing out condoms even when the whole world has gone gray, and when there aren't even enough women left to work the salt mines.

UNFPA is a $395 million-dollar agency that funds "family planning" programs around the world. Its chief clients are branches of the International Planned Parenthood Federation—the largest abortion-provider in the world—and such unsavory population controllers as the Chinese government. The only way to stop UNFPA is to dry up its funding. A small but necessary first step would be to ensure that UNFPA gets at most $21 million dollars of our money, rather than $37 million.

"The United Nations is on record all over the place as opposing . . . forced sterilizations and abortions."

The United States Is Not Justified in Withdrawing Funds from United Nations' Population Control Programs

Ellen Goodman

In the following viewpoint Ellen Goodman maintains that withdrawing U.S. support from the United Nations Population Fund (UNFPA) is not justified as a method of preventing coerced abortions in China. Goodman argues that current laws prevent U.S. money from being used to fund abortions overseas. Therefore, withholding U.S. funds from UNFPA means that there will be less money available to pay for midwives, hospitals, and contraception, and thus thousands of poor women throughout the world will suffer and die. Ellen Goodman is a nationally syndicated columnist and author.

As you read, consider the following questions:

1. According to Ellen Goodman, what is the UN position on forced sterilizations and abortions?
2. What does Goodman argue the UNFPA has done in China?
3. In the author's opinion, what is the problem with giving the UNFPA money to the United States Agency for International Aid (USAID)?

O ver the years, I thought my mind had become boggle-proof.

It's a side effect of journalism. Sooner or later, we just lose the ability to be astonished by anything the government says. We lose the capacity to be overwhelmed by even the most nimble political spin. But the Bush administration challenged all my insulation this week [late July 2002] when it withheld $34 million in international family planning funds designated for the United Nations.

The stated reason—and I use the word "reason" loosely—is that the UN's population fund (UNFPA) works in China. Any money to the agency, it said, helps the "Chinese government to implement more effectively its programs of coercive abortion."

Prohibited by Law

Well, allow me to explain the circuit breaker on outrage. None of the money we give to the population fund could go to China anyway.

It's against the law. It's also against the law for any U.S. money to fund abortions overseas. I know this and so do the folks in the Bush administration. Worst of all, and here's the clincher, they also know that the United Nations is not part of the problem of Chinese coercive policies; it's part of the solution.

Nevertheless, [U.S. secretary of state] Colin Powell, acting as front man for the White House, wrote, "If there is a single principle that unifies Americans with conflicting views on the subject, it is the conviction that no woman should be forced to have an abortion." True enough. But Powell failed to mention that this single principle also unifies the United Nations.

The United Nations is on record all over the place as opposing the forced sterilizations and abortions that have too often accompanied China's one-child policy. It spends only $3.5 million of a $270-million budget in the People's Republic, but it is spent in 32 counties in a deliberate effort to show the Chinese government that voluntary family planning works.

"Here are the horrible things we've done in China," says

the Fund's Sarah Craven with a good deal of restraint. "We've published materials letting the Chinese know the rights they have under UN human rights treaties. We've contracted to train family planning workers on quality care and informed consent.

"We've paid so Chinese family planning workers can go to other countries and see how it works. And we have a women's empowerment initiative to work on literacy and health care."

Many Will Die

All told, the U.N. estimates that by withholding once promised funds, the new anti-UNFPA policy will result in 2 million unwanted pregnancies, 4,800 maternal deaths, 77,000 more deaths among children under the age of 5 and almost 1 million abortions.

Thoraya Obaid, executive director of UNFPA, said plainly, "Women and children will die because of this decision."

Niek Biegman, a former Dutch ambassador to NATO [the North Atlantic Treaty Organization] who investigated UNFPA work in China, expressed dismay as to why Bush would cave to the unfounded concerns of the Religious Right.

"It's not really understood by the rest of the world how a superpower like America can be influenced in such a deadly way by four or five fanatics," Biegman [said]. "It's amazing."

"House Vote on United Nations Population Fund Is a Genuine Tragedy," www.thecarpetbaggerreport.com, July 16, 2003.

Indeed—and here comes another boggle—the rate of abortion has decreased in the places where the United Nations has worked. "We're there to give the women of China hope," Craven concludes.

Remember last year when the secretary of state praised the UNFPA's "invaluable work" around the world? Since then, a team of British parliamentarians, including an ardent pro-life leader, went to China and concluded that the UNFPA was a force for positive change. Since then, a three-member team sent by our government also gave the United Nations a clean report card.

But in an act of public humiliation worthy of Mao's Red Guard, Powell was forced to publicly recant and deliver the party line of the right wing.

The Two-China Policy

No one is making light of coercion in China. Certainly not those who believe in a woman's right to decide. But it's fair to ask whether we change policy best by engaging or disengaging with another government.

Just last month [June 2002], Health and Human Services Secretary Tommy Thompson proudly announced that we would work with China—indeed with the same health ministry that administers population policies—on issues of HIV-AIDS.

Meanwhile, we sign trade agreements and explore closer military ties. Has the old two-China policy morphed into a new two-China policy? One for family planning and one for everything else? The Bush administration says it will give the family planning money to our own Agency for International Development. Fine. But let's remember that USAID operates in 84 countries, compared with the UNFPA's 140. It operates unilaterally. And why, by the way, do we need to replicate programs in, say, Afghanistan?

This is the story. In an effort to punish China, the same China that we engage with every day, we are going to withhold money, which wouldn't go to China anyway, from the rest of the world's women.

As Amy Coen of Population Action International says, "This is the man who supports women's rights? This administration is placating and throwing red meat to a political base that doesn't believe in family planning."

Two Million Unwanted Pregnancies

Follow the bouncing boggle: In an effort to punish a UN operation that "gives hope to women in China," we are going to withdraw $34 million that pays for midwives and hospitals, birthing kits and contraceptives. And to appease the domestic "right-to-life" lobby, we are going to withhold enough money to prevent 2 million unwanted pregnancies, 4,700 maternal deaths and more than 77,000 infant and child deaths.

If Bush gets away with this one, I'm definitely gonna take myself in for some new boggle-proofing.

Periodical Bibliography

The following articles have been selected to supplement the diverse views presented in this chapter.

Antoaneta Bezlova   "China to Formalize One-Child Policy," *Asia Times*, May 24, 2001.

Johanna Brenner   "Transnational Feminism and the Struggle for Global Justice," *New Politics*, Winter 2003.

Pete Dygert   "Prosperity and Population Control," *Clarion*, February 11, 2000.

EngenderHealth   "Contraceptive Sterilization: Executive Summary," 2004. www.engenderhealth.org.

Christopher Farrell   "The Not-So-High Cost of Aging," *Business Week Online*, July 16, 2004. www. businessweek.com.

Aliette Frank   "Conservations Focus on Population Growth," *National Geographic News*, April 17, 2001.

Laura L. Garcia   "The Globalization of Family Planning," *World & I*, December 2000.

Adrienne Germain   "First Empower," *Our Planet*, 2004.

Michael Hagmann   "The World in 2050: More Crowded, Urban, and Aged," *Bulletin of the World Health Organization*, May 2001.

Christine L. Himes   "Age 100 and Counting," Population Reference Bureau, April 2003. www.prb.org.

Don Hinrichsen   "China's Quiet Revolution in Reproductive Health," January 7, 2004. www. peopleandplanet.net.

John Knodel and Mary Beth Ofstedal   "Gender and Aging in the Developing World," *Population and Development Review*, December 2003.

Ellen Lukas   "How the UN Is Exploiting the Population Issue," *Crisis*, September 1, 2003.

Steven W. Mosher   "Graduating Countries from Population Control," *Catholic Exchange*, September 30, 2002.

Steven W. Mosher   "Their Appointed Rounds," *PRI Weekly Briefing*, March 2, 2001.

Ann Noonan   "One-Child Crackdown," *National Review*, August 16, 2001.

Population Action
International
"What Is International Population Assistance?"
February 2, 2002. www.populationaction.org.

Lisa Ann Richey
"Why Demographic Fatigue Contributes Little
to Our Understanding of Contemporary
Africa," Population and Development
Program, Hampshire College, Spring 2000.
www.clpp.hampshire.edu.

Bruce Sundquist
"The Controversy Over U.S. Support for
International Family Planning: An Analysis,"
August 2004. www.home.alltel.net.

Time
"Twilight of the Boomers," June 12, 2000.

For Further Discussion

Chapter 1

1. Austin Ruse argues that rich nations are trying to reduce the populations in poor nations through coerced contraception, abortion, and sterilization. In your opinion, do more affluent nations have the right to intervene in the population policies of poor nations? Why or why not?

2. Nicholas Eberstadt argues that human beings have the capacity for solving problems by changing their environment. He cites scientific discoveries that have greatly increased food production as evidence that increasing population density will not result in widespread famine. In your opinion, is the capacity to solve population problems scientifically without bounds? For example, can food production be increased indefinitely? Explain.

Chapter 2

1. Don Hinrichsen and Bryant Robey argue that large population increases are destroying the earth. Betsy Hartmann insists that population increases and the countries where they occur are not to blame for the degradation of the earth—poverty is the real culprit. In your opinion, are ecological challenges economic problems or population problems? Explain, citing the viewpoints.

2. The earth can no longer produce enough food for all the people living on it, Geoffrey Lean contends. He argues that slowing population growth is the answer to hunger. However, editors at Pregnant Pause insist that there is plenty of food available now and that with the help of technology, the earth is capable of producing even more. Thus, overpopulation is not a cause of hunger and there is no need to be concerned with population growth. In your opinion, does the production of enough food necessarily ensure that no one will be hungry? Explain.

3. Niles Eldredge claims that ecological stress from human overpopulation is pushing humanity toward extinction. Fred Pearce argues that it is not overpopulation but a steadily declining population that is endangering humans. Why is it significant that most of the countries with declining populations are in developed areas of the world—countries that also use the most resources?

Chapter 3

1. Edward Tabash argues that a high immigration rate is the main cause of U.S. population increases and the problems that accompany it. Daniel T. Griswold maintains that newborn babies—not

immigrants—account for U.S. population increases, and that immigrants are unfairly blamed for many problems. In your opinion, would better management of growth and existing resources help solve population problems without the necessity of limiting immigration? Explain, citing from the viewpoints.

2. Steve Gill insists that increased immigration is to blame for U.S. unemployment and low wages for unskilled workers. Michael Tanner argues that immigration has little negative effect on unemployment or wages, and actually helps create jobs. In your opinion, should immigration into the United States be limited only to those individuals who possess skills and experience that American workers cannot provide? Explain.

3. Rob Sobhani maintains that large population increases resulting from immigration are undermining national unity. Henry Cisneros, however, contends that a large immigrant influx does not necessarily undermine national unity. In your opinion, would the population problem be solved by limiting the total number of immigrants or just immigrants from certain countries? Explain.

Chapter 4

1. K. Prasada Rao argues that the government of the state of Andhra Pradesh in India should encourage population control to promote economic growth. Christopher Lingle argues that population control is misguided and contends that governments should concentrate on economic policies to encourage growth. Do you think governments ever have the right to intervene to either encourage or discourage population growth? Explain, citing the viewpoints.

2. Amit Sen Gupta insists that economic development, not aggressive or coercive population control, is the fastest way for India to advance economically. Carol A. Kates claims that population control is necessary for economic advancement to occur. Which argument is stronger? Why?

3. The Society for the Protection of Unborn Children argues that pro-lifers in the West should pressure the Chinese government to abolish the one-child policy. In your opinion, should foreigners have a voice in the policies of the Chinese government? Explain.

4. Austin Ruse and Douglas A. Sylva insist that the UN Population Division's report proves that despite population growth, the situation of poor people throughout the world has improved due to a decrease in poverty and an increase in food production. In your opinion, does this mean that population control is no longer necessary? Explain.

Organizations to Contact

The editors have compiled the following list of organizations concerned with the issues debated in this book. The descriptions are derived from materials provided by the organizations. All have publications or information available for interested readers. The list was compiled on the date of publication of the present volume; the information provided here may change. Be aware that many organizations take several weeks or longer to respond to inquiries, so allow as much time as possible.

Carrying Capacity Network (CCN)
2000 P St., Suite 310, Washington, DC 20036
(202) 296-4548 • fax: (202) 296-4609
e-mail: carryingcapacity@covad.net
Web site: www.carryingcapacity.org

CCN is concerned about world population issues and disseminates information to other organizations working on issues related to the earth's carrying capacity. It publishes the *Immigration Briefing Book;* the bimonthly *Clearinghouse Bulletin*, which includes environmental legislation updates; and the quarterly *Focus*, which provides in-depth coverage of current environmental issues.

Human Life International (HLI)
4 Family Ln., Front Royal, VA 22630-6453
(561) 635-7884 • fax: (561) 635-7363
e-mail: hli@hli.org • Web site: www.hli.org

HLI is a pro-life religious organization that opposes international population control efforts. It rejects the idea that overpopulation is a problem, and instead supports education, coupled with more humane governmental and economic policies, as the best solution to world hunger and environmental damage. Its monthly newsletter, *HLI Reports*, contains many articles on population control.

International Women's Health Coalition (IWHC)
24 E. Twenty-first St., New York, NY 10010
(212) 979-8500 • fax: (212) 979-9009
e-mail: info@iwhc.org • Web site: www.iwhc.org

IWHC supports women's reproductive health in the developing world via innovative health-care programs and policy research. It offers educational materials on reproductive health and copublished the "Rio Statement" to represent a feminist position at the 1994 UN Conference on Population and Development held in Cairo, Egypt.

Negative Population Growth (NPG)
2861 Duke St., Alexandria, VA 22314
(703) 370-9510 • fax: (703) 370-9514
e-mail: npg@npg.org • Web site: www.npg.org

NPG is concerned with population and environmental issues and works to promote a decrease in U.S. and world populations. It publishes a triannual newsletter, *Human Survival*, as well as various position papers, including *Zero Net Migration*, *Beyond Family Planning*, and *Family Responsibility*.

Population Action International (PAI)
1300 Nineteenth St. NW, Second Fl., Washington, DC 20036
(202) 557-3400 • fax: (202) 728-4177
e-mail: pai@popact.org • Web site: www.populationaction.org

PAI concentrates on policies and programs that down the world's population by stressing the education of women and the voluntary use of contraceptive devices. It gives annual "Picks and Pans" awards to ten countries with the best and worst population programs.

Population Connection
1400 Sixteenth St. NW, Suite 320, Washington, DC 20036
(202) 332-2200 • fax: (202) 332-2302
e-mail: info@populationconnection.org
Web site: www.populationconnection.org

Previously known as Zero Population Growth (ZPG), Population Connection works to slow population growth and achieve a sustainable balance of population, resources, and the environment. Its education and advocacy programs aim to influence public policies, attitudes, and behavior on national and global population issues and related concerns. It publishes reports and activist kits on issues such as women's access to reproductive services, population and the environment, and religious opposition to population control.

The Population Council
One Dag Hammerskjold Plaza, New York, NY 10017
(212) 339-0500 • fax: (212) 755-6052
e-mail: pubinfo@popcouncil.org • Web site: www.popcouncil.org

The council conducts research on social science, biomedicine, and public health in order to improve the well-being and reproductive health of people living in developing nations. Its numerous publications include the quarterly *Population Development Review*; the bimonthly *Studies in Family Planning*; and books such as *Resources, Environment, and Population* and *The New Politics of Population*.

The Population Institute
107 Second St. SE, Washington, DC 20002
(202) 544-3300
Web site: www.populationinstitute.org
The Population Institute is an international organization concerned with the consequences of rapid population growth. It works to build awareness about overpopulation and advocates for measures to help stabilize population. It publishes the bimonthly newsletter *Popline* and the yearly report *World Population Overview*.

Population Reference Bureau
1875 Connecticut Ave. NW, Suite 520, Washington, DC 20009
(800) 877-9881 • fax: (202) 328-3937
e-mail: popref@prb.org • Web site: www.prb.org
The Population Reference Bureau serves as a source for population statistics in the United States and the world. It publishes current data, identifies trends, and makes projections. The bureau publishes the quarterly *Population Bulletin*, the monthly *Population Today*, and U.S. and world population data sheets.

Population Research Institute (PRI)
PO Box 1559, 1190 Progress Dr., Suite 2D, Front Royal, VA 22630
(540) 622-5240 • fax: (540) 622-2728
e-mail: pri@pop.org • Web site: www.pop.org
PRI is a nonprofit educational organization that opposes population control programs that do not respect the dignity and rights of individuals and families. PRI works to document abuses of human rights in the name of population control, and to promote the material and social benefits of moderate population growth. It publishes the newsletter *PRI Review* and special publications such as *Know Your Rights!* and *The Facts of Global Depopulation*.

United Nations Population Fund (UNFPA)
220 East Forty-second St., New York, NY 10017 212-297-5020
e-mail: hetle@unfpa.org • Web site: www.unfpa.org
UNFPA is the largest internationally funded source of population assistance to developing countries. The fund assists developing countries, at their request, in ensuring access to reproductive health services and in devising population and development strategies. It also works to raise awareness of these issues in all countries. Its publications include *6 Billion: A Time for Choices* and the yearly *State of the World Population*.

Worldwatch Institute
1776 Massachusetts Ave. NW, Washington, DC 20036-1904
(202) 452-1999 • fax: (202) 296-7365
e-mail: worldwatch@worldwatch.org
Web site: www.worldwatch.org
Worldwatch Institute is an interdisciplinary research organization that works to inform policy makers and the public about global and environmental issues. It publishes the bimonthly *WorldWatch* magazine, periodic *Worldwatch Papers*, and the annual *State of the World* report.

Bibliography of Books

Nancy Birdsall et al. *Population Matters: Demographic Change, Economic Growth, and Poverty in the Developing World.* New York: Oxford University Press, 2003.

Lester Russell Brown *Plan B: Rescuing a Planet Under Stress and a Civilization in Trouble.* New York: Norton, 2003.

Patrick J. Buchanan *The Death of the West: How Dying Populations and Immigrant Invasions Imperil Our Country and Civilization.* New York: Thomas Dunne Books, 2001.

Stephen Castles and Mark J. Miller *The Age of Migration, Third Edition: International Population Movements in the Modern World.* New York: Guilford, 2003.

Paul R. Ehrlich and Anne H. Ehrlich *One with Nineveh: Politics, Consumption, and the Human Future.* Washington, DC: Island Press/ Shearwater Books, 2004.

John Firor and Judith Jacobsen *The Crowded Greenhouse: Population, Climate Change, and Creating a Sustainable World.* New Haven, CT: Yale University Press, 2002.

Robert William Fogal et al. *The Escape from Hunger and Premature Death, 1700–2100: Europe, America, and the Third World.* Cambridge, UK: Cambridge University Press, 2004.

Lev Ginzburg et al. *Ecological Orbits: How Planets Move and Populations Grow.* New York: Oxford University Press, 2004.

Lindsey Grant *Too Many People: The Case for Reversing Growth.* Santa Ana, CA: Seven Locks Press, 2000.

Victor Davis Hanson *Mexifornia: A State of Becoming.* San Francisco: Encounter Books, 2003.

James E. Harf and Mark Owen Lombardi, eds. *Taking Sides: Clashing Views on Controversial Global Issues.* Guilford, CT: Dushkin/McGraw-Hill, 2001.

Paul Harrison et al. *AAAS Atlas of Population and Environment.* Berkeley: University of California Press, 2000.

Leonard G. Horowitz *Death in the Air: Globalism, Terrorism, and Toxic Warfare.* Sandpoint, ID: Tetrahedron, 2001.

Valerie M. Hudson and Andrea M. den Boer *Bare Branches: The Security Implications of Asia's Surplus Male Population.* Cambridge, MA: The MIT Press, 2004.

Samuel P. Huntington	*Who We Are: The Challenges to America's National Identity.* New York: Simon & Schuster, 2004.
Tamar Jocoby	*Reinventing the Melting Pot: New Immigrants and What It Means to Be American.* Boulder, CO: Basic Books, 2004.
Karen Kasmauski	*Impact: Dispatches from the Front Lines of Global Health.* Washington, DC: National Geographic, 2003.
Klaus M. Leisinger et al.	*Six Billion and Counting: Population Growth and Food Security in the 21st Century.* Washington, DC: International Food Policy Research Institute, 2002.
Phillip Longman	*The Empty Cradle: How Falling Birthrates Threaten World Prosperity and What to Do About It.* Boulder, CO: Basic Books, 2004.
Wolfgang Lutz et al.	*The End of World Population Growth in the 21st Century.* London, UK: Earthscan, 2004.
Diane J. Macunovich	*Birth Quake: The Baby Boom and Its Aftershocks.* Chicago: University of Chicago Press, 2002.
Jeffrey Kevin McKee	*Sparing Nature: The Conflict Between Human Population Growth and Earth's Biodiversity.* New Brunswick, NJ: Rutgers University Press, 2003.
Donella H. Meadows	*The Limits to Growth: The 30-Year Update.* White River Junction, VT: Chelsea Green, 2004.
Phillip Musgrove	*Health Economics in Development.* Washington, DC: World Bank, 2004.
Vicente Narvarro and Carles Muntaner	*Political and Economic Determinants of Population Health and Well-Being: Controversies and Developments.* Amityville, NY: Baywood Publishing, 2004.
K. Bruce Newbold	*Six Billion Plus: Population Issues in the Twenty-First Century.* Lanham, MD: Rowman and Littlefield, 2002.
Brian C. O'Neill et al.	*Population and Climate Change.* Cambridge, UK: Cambridge University Press, 2001.
Xizhe Peng et al.	*The Changing Population of China.* Malden, MA: Blackwell, 2000.
Thomas Scharping	*Birth Control in China 1949–2000: Population Policy and Demographic Development.* New York: Routledge, 2002.

William Stanton | *The Rapid Growth of Human Populations 1750–2000: Histories, Consequences, Issues, Nation by Nation.* Brentwood Essex, UK: Multi-Science, 2004.

United States Congressional Executive Commission on China | *Women's Rights and China's New Family Planning Law.* Washington, DC: U.S. Government Printing Office, 2002.

Jay Weinstein and Vijayan K. Pillai | *Demography: The Science of Population.* Needham Heights, MA: Allyn and Bacon, 2000.

Index